Cambridge Elements

Elements in Magic
edited by
Marion Gibson
University of Exeter

AMULETS IN MAGICAL PRACTICE

Jay Johnston
University of Sydney

Shaftesbury Road, Cambridge CB2 8EA, United Kingdom

One Liberty Plaza, 20th Floor, New York, NY 10006, USA

477 Williamstown Road, Port Melbourne, VIC 3207, Australia

314–321, 3rd Floor, Plot 3, Splendor Forum, Jasola District Centre, New Delhi – 110025, India

103 Penang Road, #05–06/07, Visioncrest Commercial, Singapore 238467

Cambridge University Press is part of Cambridge University Press & Assessment, a department of the University of Cambridge.

We share the University's mission to contribute to society through the pursuit of education, learning and research at the highest international levels of excellence.

www.cambridge.org
Information on this title: www.cambridge.org/9781009517799

DOI: 10.1017/9781108953412

When citing this work, please include a reference to the DOI 10.1017/9781108953412

First published 2024

A catalogue record for this publication is available from the British Library.

ISBN 978-1-009-51779-9 Hardback
ISBN 978-1-108-94879-1 Paperback
ISSN 2732-4087 (online)
ISSN 2732-4079 (print)

Amulets in Magical Practice

Elements in Magic

DOI: 10.1017/9781108953412
First published online: March 2024

Jay Johnston
University of Sydney

Author for correspondence: Jay Johnston, jay.johnston@sydney.edu.au

Abstract: This Element takes as its remit the production and use of amulets. The focus will be on amulets with no, or minimal, textual content like those comprising found stone, semi-precious gems, and/ or animal body parts. That is, a material form that is unaccompanied by directive textual inscription. The analysis considers this materiality to understand its context of use including ritual and metaphysical operations. Through discussion of selected case studies from British, Celtic, and Scandinavian cultures, it demonstrates the associative range of meaning that enabled the attribution of power/agency to the amuletic object. Uniquely, it will consider this material culture from an interdisciplinary perspective, drawing together insights from the disciplines of cultural studies, religious studies, folklore studies, archaeology, and Scandinavian studies. It develops the concept of 'trans-aniconism' to encapsulate an amulet's temporal relations and develops the proposition of 'landscape amulets'.

Keywords: amulet, materiality, vernacular, belief, magic

ISBNs: 9781009517799 (HB), 9781108948791 (PB), 9781108953412 (OC)
ISSNs: 2732-4087 (online), 2732-4079 (print)

Contents

Introduction

> Ritual can be both sacred and secular – it does not have to be either/or – and so an object can be both numinous and profane.
>
> Hall, 2021: 487

Over the past decade there has been an astounding shift in what can be said in academic discourse about material agency and ontology. That is, the proposition that material substances are not inert brute matter but, rather, have their own volition and affect. The work of Karen Barad (2007) on agential realism and Jane Bennett (2010) on vibrant matter have been dominating discourses, providing academics in a wide variety of disciplines with a respectable language with which to speak about the other-than-human agencies of matter with legitimacy for doing so. This Element is similarly concerned with material agencies, particularly those not ascribed to human volition and which trouble modern ontological boundaries. However, herein the conceptual framework is drawn from discourses and worldviews long ridiculed in the academy (even taking the recent thaw towards the topic into account). Quite simply, these frameworks are found within spiritual or esoteric worldviews rather than secular conceptual fields, albeit religious nomenclature does seep into the secular prescription as well. It is these esoteric frameworks that have been, and continue to be, employed to understand the agency and ontology of amulets.

This Element takes as its remit amulets with no, or minimal, textual content. For example, those comprising carved stone, semi-precious gems, and animal body parts (feathers, beaks, claws, etc.). That is, a material form that is unaccompanied by directive textual inscription, sigils, or visual talismans. It also largely excludes wholly human-crafted artefacts, for example, small 'Thor's Hammer' charms cast in metal. However, worked materials such as carved wood and shell do make an appearance in one example. In the consideration of such material culture, the materiality of the object is therefore key to understanding the amulet's context of use and its ritual and metaphysical operations. Through a discussion of selected case studies drawn from British and Scandinavian cultures, this analysis will explain and demonstrate the associative range of meanings that enabled the attribution of power/agency to the amuletic object (and where relevant, how and when such meanings changed). It approaches this material from an interdisciplinary perspective, drawing together insights from a variety of disciplines, especially religious studies, anthropology, 'folk' (vernacular) studies, cultural studies (particularly medical history), archaeology, and Scandinavian studies. This discussion sets these worldviews and interpretations in dialogue with the recent ontological turn. In its fullness of exploration, this Element asks an overarching question regarding whether 'magical' practice requires reconceptualisation within such a context.

What constitutes 'magical practice' whilst sounding straightforward enough remains a vexed question. The study of magic is itself beset by definitional disputes and quandaries, albeit it continues to receive sustained academic analysis (for a short overview, see, Johnston, 2022). In a reductive characterisation it is suffice to account for it herein as a worldview in which other-than-human agencies are recognised and are considered, via specific practices, capable of being manipulated by human intention. So too, those same other-than-human agencies are understood as equally capable of affecting humans according to their own intent. The way in which such relation is achieved is provided by the foundational worldview of the specific culture or belief system, many of which challenge modern empirical ontological divisions. This is a necessarily general characterisation of magic that the following discussion seeks to illustrate, via specific examples which demonstrate the diversity of how these relations and material ontologies are conceptualised. In some cases, 'magic' may not be the operative word.

It is nearly a decade since Ronald Hutton (2015) recorded that 'suddenly change is in the air' (5), describing the turn towards material culture in historical analysis and the first furtive academic explorations of ritual and/or magical material culture from medieval Christian contexts (particularly in the United Kingdom). This Element continues the trend in examination of 'magical' material culture, but does so in dialogue with the aforementioned ontological turn. Its object of study is 'amulets', a suitably troubling and slippery enough class of material culture such that an entire section – 'What Is an Amulet? Definitions and Debate' – was required to contend with it. This is followed by three sections, each of which explore a particular type of amulet, loosely based on material differences. 'Loosely' is not simply lazy category organisation on my behalf, since this Element will hopefully demonstrate that amuletic materiality often trounces typology borders. To account for this wayward behaviour Section 2 – 'Enchanted Objects: Stone Amulets' – discusses these 'rude' amulets in relation to the concept of trans-aniconism, a revision of the concept of aniconism that emphasises amulets as temporary repositories of divine agency and as mediums of transitive exchange (Johnston, 2017). The following section, 'Enchanted Beings and Their Remains: Animal Amulets', considers amulet relationality across species, multiple materials, and temporalities. The final section, 'Enchanted Places: Landscape Amulets', expands the concept and considers the proposition of collective, community amulets.

The sources for understanding an amulet's efficacy are both numerous and ephemeral. As will be demonstrated herein, antiquarian, popular discourse, and academic discussions often follow the same source material for explaining amulet selection and use. Further, vernacular knowledge, like archaeological remains, provides incomplete evidence dependent upon the collector's interest and bias, therefore, the degree of 'trustworthiness' of such material is always a factor. In a discussion of amulets in British museum collections, Tabitha Cadbury (2015) identifies a further crucial point regarding the identification of amuletic material culture, noting: 'The occultist Cecil Williamson – who moved his Museum of Witchcraft to Cornwall in 1960 – created a new context for many English amulets ... redefining them as evidence for traditional witchcraft' (194). She explains further that as popular and academic interest in magic has increased over the last decade these materials have gone through a process of being reinterpreted and returned to public display. What Cadbury's insights demonstrate is that the malleability and multiplicity of interpretative schemas are never separate from cultural, group, or individual politics and agendas. Nonetheless, these sources do provide the 'best guess' clues for the orientation and use of specific amulets and a variety will be referenced herein. An overarching concern is to illustrate the ways in which amulets are necessarily 'multi-vocal'. They 'speak' and are interpreted in many different ways simultaneously, therefore the acknowledgement and respect for plural epistemologies is requisite for their analysis and exploration.

In Europe, several significant analyses of amulets have developed from a 'collections-based approach' (Cadbury, 2015; Hukantaival, 2021). The appeal and limitations are well noted by scholars, with the 'collection' designating a grouping of material culture that, in other contexts, may be identified more prosaically. This scholarship does provide fixed dates, at least for the museum deposition of the material, but not necessarily for the amulets' productive life, and in some cases provides further familial or geographic context. Aside from the proposition of landscape amulets in Section 4, the examples discussed in this Element are from the period in western contexts between the tenth and twenty-first centuries. This encompasses the period Catherine Rider delineates for the practice of 'common magic' (eleventh to eighteenth century) (Rider, 2015: 303). As recounted by Rider (2015) the use of 'common' follows the term's use by Richard Kieckhefer (2015: 303) to designate practices that were not particular to a specific belief community but rather were generally known and could potentially have broad accessibility. This is in contradistinction to what is termed 'learned magic', which in academic studies of esotericism is associated with the practices of men of specific class and intellectual means, for example, Renaissance practitioners like Giordano Bruno. As Paola Zambelli (2007) has illuminated, the magical practices of the lower classes and/or illiterate were more commonly feminised and interpreted as 'witchcraft' (black magic) and therefore heresy. Yet both 'types' of magic share aspects of esoteric worldviews, and the delineation is most clearly a socio-cultural one. In effect, all ceremonial/ ritual magic is 'learned', and the reproduction of this binary and the privileging of certain, mostly male literate practitioners it presupposes simply continues a gendering of epistemology. The technologies and material utilised as amulets unsurprisingly reflect the material resources available to the differing classes of practitioners. Amulet use cuts across all sectors of society, incorporating the most precious of materials (jewels, for example) and the most mundane (hair, for example). Therefore the 'magical practice' of this Element's title not only encompasses those practices designated 'magic' by dominant discourses and self-labelled practitioners, it also encompasses worldviews captured by terms like 'vernacular', or 'folk belief', and even 'alternative healing'. This presupposes causal relations that are not explained by modern scientific knowledge or empirical observation. This Element does not discuss Indigenous epistemologies or what has been identified by outsiders as amulets from numerous Indigenous cultures. These are not traditions for which I am permitted to speak, and I do not wish to reappropriate or misrepresent Indigenous knowledge and worldviews. Nonetheless, developments like 'contemporary animism' are inclusive of First Nations scholars' work and will be referenced where relevant herein.

One final point remains to be made in this brief Introduction. This Element is not concerned with truth claims. Whether or not the amuletic practices discussed in this text actually 'work' is of no consequence to this discussion (it was, or still is, no doubt of quite some consequence for the amulet owner). What is crucial is the way in which the relations between the physical material and other-than-human agencies have been conceptualised and created. As will become swiftly apparent, this short Element does not seek to establish authoritative cohesion on what is a necessarily diverse and enormous subject area. Rather, it seeks to elucidate the logic(s) underpinning amulet use and to provide creative discussion of examples that are wantonly ambiguous. In doing so it also hopes to demonstrate new approaches and conceptualisations of this tricky materiality. If nothing else, amulets are at once mundane and magical.

1 What Is an Amulet? Definitions and Debate

> If we embrace ambiguity when it is present, rather than fighting it or ignoring it, focusing where necessary on the deposits 'in between' a richer account of the past will emerge.
>
> Cooper et al.: 2020: 154

In alignment with their ascribed 'otherworldly' potency, the boundaries of 'amulet' as a particular category of material culture are similarly slippery and porous. This section will introduce 'amulets' by considering standard definitions and their anomalies, and introduce themes of specific import for the argument herein, particularly issues of scale, temporality, perception, and agency. The discussion of agency will consider aspects of the recent 'ontological turn' in the humanities (including 'new materialism' and 'contemporary animism') in the context of worldviews more usually understood as esoteric or magical, and that have historically been marginalised within academic analysis. Indeed, the issue of what counts as viable knowledge – knowledge that is endorsed and valued – is crucial to understanding both the historical lack of critical engagement with amulets as objects of scholarly analysis, and the flourishing of their current appeal.

Categories for Slippery Materiality

The *Oxford English Dictionary* (2011) provides three definitions of amulet: 'Anything worn about the person as a charm or preventive against evil, mischief, disease, witchcraft, etc.'; a specifically medical usage drawn from eighteenth century sources 'Sometimes also applied … to all medicines, whether internal or external, whose virtue or manner of operation is occult', and use as a figurative expression denoting 'a preservative, protection or charm'. These three definitions, provided as they are in just a single source, summarise not only key attributes but also invoke topics and qualities of contestation. Each usage designates 'amulet' as an actant. They prevent and protect, or otherwise 'charm'. In so doing, amulets necessarily exceed the bounds of their empirical materiality, that is, whatever their physical properties, the activity of the amuletic qualities ascribed to these properties are not discernible by material science-based observation. This feature is made obvious in the *OED*'s example of medical usage that directly refers to the source of amuletic effects as 'occult', thereby designating that the source of amulets' efficacy – an element central to their categorisation – is not clearly identified or exemplified. The term 'charm' is often employed as a synonym for amulet; in recent scholarship it is commonly utilised to denote amulets that utilise words, which according to Hugh Cheape (2009: 86) follows the term's Latin etymology. However historic sources often use the terms amulet and charm interchangeably, and for this reason 'charm' is not used herein.

Collectively, the *OED*'s set of definitions is ambiguous regarding the types of material involved. The eighteenth-century medical usage implies a capacity for amulets to be digested, however, this does not necessarily equate to foodstuffs, given that ritual texts or semi-precious stones are known to have been immersed in liquid and then the liquid consumed to engender protective effect, across diverse cultural and historical periods from Ancient Egypt to eighteenth-century Britain (Beith, 2004; Pinch, 2006). What this medical example does bring to the fore is the temporal nature of some amuletic practices (the discussion of which will be a feature of later sections). So too, whilst the initial general definition of amulet is prescriptive regarding an amulet's relation to the human body – it is to be 'worn' – it is not prescriptive about its constituents. Indeed, amulets are presented as capable of being comprised of 'anything' so long as they have a capacity for wearability through which the amulet is able to form a relationship of proximity with the human body. Indeed 'amulet', as presented in the *OED* definitions presupposes a relation with an individual human subject; being physically close to its subject is requisite for efficacy. However, in other contexts the term has also been employed to characterise forms of material culture and ritual practice for which wearability is not significant.

In her discussion of modern English amulets and their materiality, Tabitha Cadbury (2015) characterises them as 'portable charms' and provides a range of examples that exhibit wearability: 'a fossil to keep away lightning, a hag stone to guard against witchcraft, a mole's foot to fight cramp' (188). Yet, they may also, Cadbury (2015) notes, be 'concealed or displayed in homes or in barns, on agricultural animals or on vehicles' (188). This summary identifies two crucial elements for any consideration of amulets. The first is the centrality of visibility, whether they were required to be 'concealed or displayed' for efficacy, and the second, the relations established with particular places, such as domestic- or work-related ('barns'), rather than individual bodies.

As such, there is a clear overlap with a type of material culture described in archaeological discourse as 'ritual deposit'. This term refers to items consciously placed in specific locations to provide protection from harmful agencies (often ascribed to a supernatural source) for those places and their inhabitants. Perhaps the most notorious examples within a modern British context are 'witch bottles'. Described as a 'uniquely British, and indeed mostly English' phenomenon (Hutton, 2015: 10) these bottles variously contain mixtures of nails, pins, hair, urine, and even animal bones that were buried or concealed within houses (Hoggard, 2015: 91–2, 101). Brian Hoggard's (2015) specific study of their historic written sources details that the bottles were designed to protect against witchcraft and were thought to 'cause pain to a witch' (102), with sympathetic association being drawn between the bottle and the witch's bladder. In contradistinction Annie Thwaite (2021: 5) interprets the textual and material sources to evidence a healing practice, arguing that their function was not purely apotropaic but rather formed a magical remedy. Therefore, as items buried in foundations or encased within walls or chimneys, for example, the bottles can be categorised as 'ritual deposit', whilst their ascribed protective function also renders them as both material remains of healing ritual and as amulets.

Whilst many scholars have noted the difficulty in identifying types of material culture deposits that can be considered 'magical' (e.g., Cummins, 2015; Hunkantaival, 2021), so too I posit that this ambiguity extends to the ascription of the term 'amulet'. In contrast to the *OED* definitions, amulets may not be small in scale or defined by wearability (Section 4 will expand on this theme). Indeed, it is useful to challenge the assumed status of an amulet as a singular object (or objects held within a singular casing, such as a bottle or a pouch). Amulets may very well be a *collection* and *arrangement* of discrete objects. The selection, placement, including concealment (or ritual deposition), of materials are potent and deliberate acts.

Certainly, the definition of an amulet need not hang purely on material objects per se, but may be considered as something other, or more-than, a single or collection of objects. This 'other' is the relations the amulet presupposes, for example a set of objects *in relation*, wherein the relations are implicit to the assigned amuletic efficacy. That is, both the objects and the relations between them form the amulet. Amulets can also be made from a collection of objects in which the relations between each are not considered of especial efficacy, but as a collection they nonetheless form the amulet. This latter sense is illustrated by Alex Owens' (2019) designation of Iron-Age hoards as 'supernatural objects', and Timothy Easton's (2015) designation 'spiritual midden' to describe household locations which have been used for the deposition of 'personal objects for spiritual reasons over a period of time', for example, chimney wells (147). Easton (2015: 162) understands the placement of such objects as apotropaic, for protection of the household, its occupants, and their industries. An important correction to this view as a default interpretative framework is supplied by Owen Davies and Ceri Houlbrook (2021: 13) in their recent volume, *Building Magic: Ritual and Re-enchantment in Post-Medieval Structures* in which they note evidence of a common builders' lark to 'brick up in walls' their companion's objects, from beer cans to newspapers and all manner of trash. Determining whether a deposit was prosaic or apotropaic is no straightforward task. Davies and Houlbrook (2021: 14–16, 73) further refine the use of ritual concealment and the concept of spiritual middens to take account of purposively sequestered items for safe-keeping, or as 'personal time-capsules' of sentiment and memory, as well as for structural reinforcement.

Debates about the correct nomenclature to describe collections of purposively concealed objects continues to be a 'site' of active archaeological enquiry. This encompasses the common terms 'ritual deposits', 'hoards', 'funerary deposits', and what Cooper et al. (2020) have called 'deposits "in-between"'. These are objects designated as funerary, albeit there are no human remains associated with their deposition, and they therefore elide standard categories of identification (Cooper et al., 2020: 153). 'Spiritual middens' and 'spiritual objects' can be considered a variant of this expression that stresses a direct association between the actual objects and some form of supernatural agency. Indeed, although Cooper et al. use 'in-between' to emphasise category ambiguity, the term is a salient moniker for all amulets. It can be taken as figuring the in-between as an active space implicit in the ascription of material potency to objects and locations (and this is not to dismiss the act of deposition from being understood as carrying its own other-than-human potency). This is the startling obvious point: that the only differentiating factor that distinguishes between an iron nail above a cradle being an amulet to ward off fairy attack – as is reported in the traditions of northern Scotland (Black, 2005) – or a functional peg upon which to hang things is the worldview through which it is perceived. Even the alternatives of purpose given in this example – the amuletic or practical – need not be an either/or choice: an iron nail could be considered both those things simultaneously. Such a dualism reproduces a common epistemological framework in dominant western discourses between the spiritual and physical – a binary that some amulets can appear to disrupt.

In the broadly western context on which this discussion is focused, materials ascribed a supranatural agency (a secular or spiritual material ontology) are considered to do so within what are designated 'magical' or ontological worldviews. This encompasses often-derided or romanticised vernacular, 'folklore', or 'traditional' knowledges. Despite their association with the historic past, these knowledges and practices are not unchanging or stable. So too, the boundaries between what is acceptable and unacceptable supranatural practice, including the identification of what is, and what is not, considered 'magic', are similarly socio-culturally constructed (Pitarakis, 2022). Although modern academic institutions have long eschewed the study of knowledges deemed occult or magical (leading one scholar notoriously describing them as 'rejected knowledges' (Hanegraaff, 2012)), many others have demonstrated that such knowledges have long accompanied, in highly entangled ways, dominant discourses including the development and practice of modern science (von Stuckrad, 2014). Ruth Barcan (2009) makes a similar observation regarding the identification of 'intuition', not only identifying several forms and variant understandings in practice, but crucially demonstrating the impossibility of claims that any such epistemology operates without an interrelationship with forms of reason and vice versa. Therefore, the identification or separation of epistemologies is not a clear-cut endeavour. The types and styles of 'knowing' which support amuletic practice are varied and include styles of logic, symbolic and associative relations, as well as foundations in specific ontological and metaphysical worldviews.

Concepts of other-than-human agency discerned in operation via various forms of materiality have received a recent resurgence in the humanities. At its most basic, this renewed focus can be understood as a continuation of the radical post-structuralist programme of decentring the human subject. Nonetheless, in order to make such concepts acceptable to the academy, and in ways that can be heard by scholars, terminology historically utilised to account for other-than-human agencies – occult, magical, supernatural, and so on – has been eschewed in favour of less spiritually loaded terms like 'vital' and 'ontological'. Indeed, the proposition of 'vital matter' can be considered a secularised form of esoteric knowledge. It is to such old and 'new materialisms' – the worldviews which underpin amulet efficacy – that this discussion now turns.

Supports for Slippery Materiality

In general – and for heuristic purposes only – an amulet's capacity to be effective can be accorded to three forms of causation (which may be concurrent):

(1) being understood to be materially comprised of a substance strongly associated, or having had direct physical contact with, a supranatural source (the cult of relics operates on a similar principle);
(2) being understood to have a symbolic or ontological relation with a supranatural source;
(3) being a focal point or embodiment of other-than-human agencies, which includes 'being' a particular deity or spirit.

Therefore, an amulet's power is considered either implicit in its materiality (often embedded in a network of symbolic or ontological relations) or the material has been made potent via some act, including modification or crafting (amulets comprised of knots, for example (Pinch, 2004: 108)). The following sections discuss examples of each. This section examines the way in which selected other-than-human agential sources have been conceptualised. It outlines two broad conceptualisations of matter: subtle matter and 'vibrant' or 'vital' matter, both which ascribe a *supra*natural agency to materiality. The term 'supranatural' is used here, rather than supernatural, as the discussion will present concepts of ontological matter developed in spiritual and secular knowledge systems. Although both terms, supernatural and supranatural, designate that which is beyond justification by empirical science, supernatural particularly evokes spooky other-worlds of spirit-beings and magic, therefore supranatural is preferred. Nonetheless, 'supranatural' is not a perfect term as it reproduces the power that the conceptualisation of 'natural' commands in dominant discourses (Asdal, 2003; Haraway, 1991). It is not used without acknowledging the important critiques of the term's socio-cultural relativity and implicit normalisation of problematic culture–nature binaries.

(i) Subtle Matter: Spiritual Agency

As a disarmingly devastating disruptor of ontological binaries, subtle matter at its most broad definition is a concept that understands the constituents of all phenomena – animal, planet, human, and so on – to be simultaneously spirit and matter (spirit–matter) or consciousness and matter (consciousness–matter). That is, it is a concept of materiality in which there is no ontological distinction posited between either 'consciousness' (or spirit) and physical material, only a scale of gradient admixtures of both. In esoteric worldviews it is this 'material' which is considered to be the fundamental constituent of all known reality, and it is often denoted with the term 'energy' or its synonyms (like vitality or liveliness). Scholarship has identified many historical and contemporary conceptualisations of subtle material with influences and correlates identified in Asian and Indigenous belief systems (albeit the resulting cultural appropriation that can occur at a popular and academic level is an issue of ethical import) (Johnston, 2008; Lockhardt, 2010; Pati and Zubko, 2020; Samuel and Johnston, 2013).

As all phenomena are considered to be comprised of subtle matter, it therefore invisibly links all 'things', and that accounts for their capacity to mutually affect one another (without any observable causation) in a complex web of lived interactions. For example, the Renaissance philosopher and physician Marsilio Ficino (1433–99) worked within the 'doctrine of signatures' system in the prescription of cures for physical ailments. Illness, thought to be the result of constitutional disharmony of the four Galenic humours of which the body was understood to be comprised (phlegmatic, melancholic, sanguine, and choleric) was alleviated through recourse to remedies that bore the 'signature' of the deficient humour (Ficino, 1996 (1489)).

This 'signature' was a constituent of the selected remedy which could variously be a combination of plant, activity, style of thought, metal, stone, animal, diet, tincture, and so on. All these disparate materials were linked in a network of invisible correspondences because they were thought to be comprised of the same ontological subtle material. All material substance was understood to derive its agency from a shared celestial subtle substance, and differing planets were distinguished by differing qualities of the subtle matter of which they were comprised. For example, someone suffering from melancholy (diseases of 'black bile') required remedies that bore the signature of Jupiter to counteract the excessive influence of the planets thought to engender the melancholic humour (Saturn and Mercury). Such remedies included: amethysts, peacocks, 'law-abiding' thoughts, and white sugar (Ficino, 1996 (1489): 90–1). Subtle matter was what constituted the correspondences between these diverse materials; at an ontological level it constituted, linked, and 'enlivened' each. The specific *qualities* of the subtle matter were determined by their particular cosmological attribution. Therefore, a vast array of diverse materiality was linked and made affective via a system of (invisible) correspondences. Systems of ontological and symbolic networks have been identified in other cultures: for example, Rune Nyord (2020) in a recent Element has claimed a network of correspondences directing the creation of images in Ancient Egypt.

Even as a mere snippet, this precis of a Renaissance system of thought exemplifies the logic in which supranatural potency is attributed to selected objects – especially that of precious and semi-precious stones, particular animal species and their by-products, and plants. It endows them with what can be considered as other-than-human amuletic qualities, although in Ficino's particular remit the focus was on healing remedies. It is also of especial note that despite being comprised *and* intersubjectively linked by the same subtle matter, individuality is not erased by subtle matter configurations. Nonetheless, distinguishing the terminus of that individuality and its agency is a much more troublesome undertaking.

I have characterised subtle matter as 'disarming' due to its popular discursive presentation in the form of subtle bodies: a conceptualisation of the self that has been core to many self-directed spiritual practices that fall under the umbrella term 'New Age' or are utilised in many forms of alternative health practices. As popular cultural practices, the belief in energetic bodies and their invisible interrelationships with all manner of material and spiritual agencies has often been met with academic derision. Subtle matter is very readily viewed as an innocuous, benign spiritual belief without its philosophical ramifications (the proposition of a radical form of intersubjectivity) being fully comprehended (Johnston, 2008). This Element is not the context in which to further extrapolate on these important ethical issues; suffice to say that ideas of invisible material agency that connect vastly different types of physical and immaterial phenomena are not new, even in forms of popular discourse. It is the association of the concept of subtle matter with worldviews other than those of dominant secular cultures – vernacular, esoteric, Indigenous, and the historically debunked – that have deemed them unpalatable. Just such a concept of matter and its ontological capacities and correspondences furnishes the logic within which amulets are potent.

(ii) Vital Matter: Secular Agency

Concepts of ontological matter, whose agency or 'aliveness' is not proposed to be derived from a spiritual or even human source, have been greatly popularised over the last decade in contemporary humanities scholarship under the umbrella label 'new materialism'. Core to much of this discussion is Jane Bennett's (2010) work on 'vital' or 'vibrant matter' and its attendant concept of 'thing-power', of which she writes: 'Thing-power gestures toward the strange ability of ordinary, man-made [*sic*] items to exceed their status as objects and to manifest traces of independence or aliveness' (xvii). This represents a view of materiality that has clear corollaries with the behaviour of amuletic material, albeit Bennett's designation is particular to human ('man')-made objects. As the previous discussion of subtle matter demonstrates, not only have esoteric knowledge systems often presupposed material agency, via concepts like subtle matter, but this agency or 'power' is attributed to a broader field of matter encompassing, for example, geology or the now inert skins and body parts of (deceased) animals. That is, the agency is not only attributed to human-worked or generated materials, but in broad terms can also be accounted for by way of the esoteric or vernacular traditions that understand these materials to *hold* valid epistemologies or potencies in and of themselves; knowledges which were sought by human subjects to be known or understood via physical proximity to the object. The amulets discussed in Sections 2 and 3 exemplify this point. Esoteric and vernacular worldviews did not limit 'liveliness' only to human-made objects.

In contradistinction to concepts like subtle matter, Bennett (2010) appears to be particularly concerned to distinguish the source of object vibrancy from anything that could be considered spiritual in nature. For example, she writes: 'I take up the hard case for a (non-mechanistic) materialism that conceives of matter as intrinsically lively (but not ensouled)' (xvii). That is, these vibrant objects are not ascribed an individualised ontological nucleus that derives its being (or becoming) from a metaphysical source. They have an agency that escapes the human – both in creation and apprehension – but this is not to be understood as the result of spiritual constituents.

Yet the discourse used to delineate vibrant matter is infused with spiritual tropes; not only the obvious reference to creating a 'kind of Nicene Creed for would-be vital materialists' (Bennett, 2010: 122), but the connotations of the term 'vibrant' itself (noting the elision between vibrant and vital that is characteristic of the discourse). Modern sensibilities might more readily associate the term 'vibrant' with a particularly outstanding quality of colour – something vivid and arresting. However, the term's etymological antecedents relate to movement: from the Latin *vibrāre* pertaining to the movement of a pendulum or oscillation. Use denoting movement is recorded from 1616, whilst association with a particular quality of colour or luminosity is not recorded until 1971 (OED, 2021: n.p.). This association with a quality of movement finds a corollary with subtle matter, whose degrees of spiritual refinement are often described via a temporal scale. For example, discourses of the modern Theosophists identify between seven varieties of subtle material, each distinguished from one another by their rates of vibration. Increased rates of vibration denote ever-subtler forms of subtle matter (Gawain, 1978: 6), an 'internal' temporality exhibited by the capacity for movement signalling agency. So too, any split between the visual and kinetic connotations of 'vibrant' is ambiguous given the long historical association of luminosity with spiritual refinement. This correlation is perhaps particularly worthy of further reflection given Michael Taussig's (2009) argument that the colonial West has an aversion to bright 'vivid' colour.

Over a decade later, since the 2010s, the concept of vibrant matter has been adopted and applied to analysis in many knowledge fields, including archaeology and material culture studies (e.g., Cipolla, 2018; Crellin et al., 2020; Govier and Steel, 2021; Jones, 2017; Lindstrøm, 2015). Other attendant fields have also enquired into this interest in secular vibrant matter: the visual arts, religious studies, archaeology, anthropology, and – drawing particularly on the work of Alfred Gell (1998) and David Freedberg (1989) – into material agency being 'operationalised' by iconography and image-making practices (cf. Garrow and Gosden, 2021; Johnston, 2010, 2016, 2020). As a result, interpretations have developed that strongly align with esoteric worldviews (what I have elsewhere referred to as an esoteric aesthetics) which render image and iconography as visual invocations, especially when they take the form of talisman or sigil 'diagram' that becomes a type of perpetual prayer or protective 'spell' embodied in the material image. Talismans and sigils have a long history of use as amulets, including in European medical practice up until the seventeenth century (Cummings, 2015). This Element's focus, however, is firmly on objects in which iconographic detail is either entirely absent or else far from a dominant feature – amulets whose efficacy is primarily mediated by their 'rude' materiality.

(iii) Agential Realism and Material Culture

The ontological elisions that are foundational to concepts of subtle matter find a corollary with Karen Barad's (2007) proposition regarding the mutual imbrication of knowledge and matter. Generated within the field of philosophy of science, particularly theoretical physics, and feminist theory, Barad's discussion of 'agential realism' has been an important factor in the development of 'new materialism'. In a consideration of prehistoric materiality Andrew Merion Jones makes clear the utility of Barad's (2012) work for analysing material culture: 'Plainly stated, the ways in which we describe the world (and the apparatus we use to describe it) are mutually related. We cannot describe the world without acting on it and shaping it' (13). Quoting Barad directly, Jones (2012) highlights her definition of matter, which is a direct correlate to that of subtle matter, the conceptualisation of matter that has furnished the innumerable logics which account for the operations of magic and the potency of amulets. 'Matter is "both produced and productive, generated and generative." For Barad, humans and matter are caught up in mutual performances as agents which bring each other into being' (13).

Whilst this conceptualisation opens a plethora of correlate philosophical propositions (even from just within the western tradition) and a much more detailed account of the way in which conceptualisations of subtle matter evince similar inter-dependent agential processes (see Johnston, 2008), such discussions would lead too far away from the amulets per se. Nonetheless, the relevance of Barad's agential realism and its take up in archaeology for a consideration of amulets is the emphasis placed on *observation*. How we perceive – our practices of perception – are not simple acts of apprehending 'what is out there', they are part of a mutual subject–object interrelationship. Importantly, following Bennett's work on vibrant matter, Jones (2013) notes the centrality of human perception to Barad's theory of world-creating mutual imbrication of action–perception. Indeed, how to account for material liveliness that does not 'impinge upon the human world' is the focus of his analysis (14). Similarly, this is a concern that haunts any consideration of amulets, especially when they are specifically deposited and/or when the amulet comprises several discrete material parts 'working' in unison (for example, the witches' bottles previously discussed). For whose 'eyes' are they constructed? What perceptive modalities do they privilege? This is the topic for the next and final part of this section.

Although the concepts of material agency discussed have been labelled 'spiritual' and 'secular', it is to be noted that this is not necessarily a clear-cut division (no matter how much that unsettles the critical theorists). Indeed, in the slippery – and largely invisible – world of agential materialism the neat divide between any binary category is at the very least unstable. As has also been noted, discursive tropes also slip across the spiritual–secular divide; a divide that is of no utility in many worldviews. Decolonising knowledge includes troubling the binaries which structure dominant worldviews, and as the development of 'contemporary animism' has attested (Harvey, 2014), there are many Indigenous cultures within a broader European context in which forms of relational ontology and material agency are implicit to their worldview.

As has been implicit in the discussion above, any conceptualisation of a supranatural matter, subtle, vital, or otherwise, is founded upon the fallibility of empirical methods of human apprehension to account for the complexity of material interaction in their subtlety and entirety. It is to the critical role played by perception that the final part of this initial section turns.

Epistemologies for Slippery Materiality

Attendant to the concepts of agential matter so far discussed is the accompanying conundrum of how these vibrant material agencies are to be perceived, given that the entirety of their activity is presented as beyond apprehension by empirical methods. The esoteric traditions within which ideas of subtle matter are found privilege the development of 'alternate' perceptive skills, those that might otherwise be termed intuitive or be denoted by terms like extra-sensory or psychic senses. Indeed, certain types of amulets have been attributed with the capacity to bestow such 'sixth senses' upon their user. The bored stone of the seventh-century Scottish prophet (more likely a legendary rather than historical figure) the Brahan Seer Kenneth Mackenzie, being a notorious example. His skills in the 'second sight' were understood to be activated by peering through the centre-hole of a stone especially gifted to him (Henderson and Cowan, 2007, 2011 [2001]: 93).

In a secular context to perceive material agency, Bennett (2010) has advocated for the development of a 'naïve ambition' to allow oneself to be 'temporarily infected by discredited philosophies of nature', including practices deemed superstition (17). As I have discussed elsewhere (Johnston, 2016b), these are ethically difficult terms to countenance if referring to vernacular, esoteric, or Indigenous worldviews, about which there is nothing naïve (and the contagion metaphor is inappropriate at best). However, cultivating naïvety may have some validity if the term is employed to capture an openness to enquiry, curiosity, and humility.

Esoteric traditions propose many different forms of body–mind practice aimed at the cultivation of perception, that is, developing extra-sensory skills to discern the operations of otherwise invisible, subtle matter. So too, vernacular traditions record practices of sensory attunement that some scholars have aligned with shamanic practice (Wilby, 2013). Alongside an understanding that such skills could be developed is the belief that they are innate, with certain families or individuals understood as being born with, or inheriting, extra-sensory skills. The study of these 'extra-sensory' skills has long been a feature of scholarship; for example, Robert Boyle the renowned early historian of science undertook a sustained study of second sight in Scotland of the eighteenth century, featuring the Revd. Robert Kirk of fairy faith fame (Hunter, 2001). Eschewing truth claim frameworks, more recent sensory studies have taken a culturally specific approach to investigating 'sixth senses' (Howes, 2009).

So too, the turn towards relational ontologies ('contemporary animism' for example), inclusive of many different Indigenous worldviews, necessitates the consideration of many different styles of knowledge (feelings, intuition, visions, etc.) often founded on the cultivation of sensory perception. It should be remembered that the epistemological divisions given here are those constructed in dominant western knowledge systems and likely have no relevance for understanding knowledge formation in Indigenous cultures. The divisions are more apposite for vernacular traditions that are inherently part of western knowledge systems.

In the consideration of amulets, the elusive agencies deemed tricky of discernment by empirical means are intertwined with more tangible physical qualities, like texture and colour. These attributes are often important for understanding the amulet's selection and utilisation. That is, they are important factors in any logic of correspondences that intimately associates the amulet with particular supranatural powers. As a form of material culture, amulets are usefully analysed from archaeological perspectives. As noted, scholarship in that discipline continues to wrestle with the implications of material agency for excavation methodology and artefact analysis (see, for example, Pétursdóttir, 2012). Contemporary archaeology has also intersected with sensory studies, with Skeates and Day (2020) providing an overview of the debates and fashions surrounding the development of sensory-focused scholarship. Unsurprisingly, they note the substantial influence of David Howes and Constance Classen (2020) on the field (2). However, not found amongst the significant publications which Skeates and Day (2009) identify and utilise is the aforementioned *Sixth Sense Reader* (albeit it is referenced in their discussion of the anthropology of colour, considered later in this section). It may still be the case that academic consideration of extra-sensory perception is more comfortably recognised in 'other' cultures (and as such, the politics of recognition carries significant ethical issues). Nonetheless, the interface of 'alternate perception' and archaeological analysis is of crucial importance for understanding the efficacy of 'rude' amulets from western cultures. 'Rude' here denotes more than simply lacking in text, although it will not be until the conclusion of this section that I further detail its proposition as a 'new' category of amulet.

Nonetheless, in taking account of 'sensory archaeology', its construction as a subfield and remit, Skeates and Day do contend with 'affect'. This is a concept that has been crucial to the formation of 'new materialism' and has allowed for the secular rendering of invisible forces and other-than-human agency (Johnston, 2021). However, in Skeates and Day's presentation, 'affect' is primarily defined by its psychological (rather than ontological) heritage. However, they acknowledge a slippage across the term's range of meaning in their edited volume, with several authors referencing Bennett's (2020) 'vibrant' materiality in their application of the term (9). In addition, Skeates and Day's survey in the field of anthropology of the senses also demonstrates that the dominant western categorisation of five senses and their physiological alignment (for example, eyes–vision, hearing–ears) are culturally specific.Therefore, to understand the sensory capacities of amulets, close attention to the sensory worlds of their cultures of production is required.

The importance of portable objects and their sensory capacities is acknowledged by Skeates and Day via reference to Christopher Tilley's discussion of 'quartzite pebbles', utilised in the production of prehistoric cairns, for example, East Devon Pebbled Heaths in the UK (Skeates and Day, 2020: 9; Tilley, 2020). These rocks are interpreted as designating the supernatural via their geological materiality (a theme that forms the focus of the next section). Referencing Taussig's work on colour, Tilley writes:

> Brightly coloured things resonate of the sacred in many societies. This is a notion of colour as inherently and materially part of doing and acting, possessing magical potency and spiritual power, a bodily force to be felt rather than a matter of mere visuality. The cairn surfaces needed to retain their brilliance and vibrancy, be renewed by placing new pebbles on them . . . (Tilley, 91)

Tilley is here proposing that the colour of the stones is implicit to their spiritual agency. Colour here is an *agency*, not a mere inert quality of the object, and further – as with many epistemologies associated with modes of supranatural perception – it is not only to be associated with one modality of perception (in this case vision). The pebbles' placement on the cairn is no doubt deliberate, but an attendant question is whether in considering Tilley's argument they should be considered amulets. This case study has been selected to exemplify the inherent intersubjectivity of colour–matter–agency. Considering the apprehension and role of material agency is not only about endeavouring to seize flickers of agency exceeding any material form, it also requires considering the qualities of the material itself from a broad range of perceptive perspectives in addition to that of empirical observation.

In a consideration of the dynamics of light on archaeological interpretation, Marion Dowd (2020) identifies a range of sensory perceptions in addition to the privileged five, all of which she assures the reader are 'accepted amongst neurologists':

> . . . *thermoception* (the experience of heat and cold); *nociception* (the unconscious perception of physical pain); *equilibrioception* (awareness of the body's position and acceleration); *proprioception* (perception of the physical body); *interoception* (awareness of the body's inner physiology); and *non-sense* (sensual experiences that cannot be measured or substantiated, e.g., having a 'sixth sense'). (193)

Here too, the 'sixth sense' unnerves by attracting the unfortunate moniker 'non-sense'. Even in this expanded 'set' of senses, those that elide scientific measurement are derided. 'Non-sense' seems a particularly loaded and inappropriate term; suprasensory capacities are senses and generate *in relation* experiences and knowledge that generate human worlds. As noted, the academic struggle to accommodate the existence and potential of such knowledges is now more acute in the wake of secular propositions of material agency, which by necessity evoke capacities beyond those acceptable to scientific knowledge (Johnston, 2020, 2021).

Other references to spiritual senses pertain to embodied practice of observance, including ritual practice or 'spiritual awareness' as a *sui generis* mode of knowing aligned with states of 'calm'. Dowd refers to Mary Helms' (2004) work on early Christian relationships with light and dark as implicit in the cultivation of expanded sensory awareness, noting that her work suggests 'that the sensory deprivation, exhaustion and sustained rhythmic psalmic [*sic*] chanting contributed to reduced physical drives and passions (facilitating celibacy), which in turn may have led to heightened spiritual awareness and an enhanced sense of calm' (Dowd, 2020: 198). However, the correlation between sensory deprivation and reduced 'passions' is perhaps better read as a dominant Christian trope rather than a physiological reality.

Nonetheless, the mutual imbrication of differing epistemologies and the 'sixth senses' role in subject–object relations, is not only an issue of the suitable interpretative form with which to understand objects and their sites, it is also one of practice and method. For example, Jo Day (2020) identifies Arthur Evans and

Heinrich Schliemann as two archaeologists whose practice was deeply infused by their sixth sense, noting 'Evans famously (and feverishly) dreamed of Minoans on the grand staircase at Knossos' (377). As Ruth Barcan (2009) has succinctly argued 'We spend years learning how to reason . . . Even so, no one, when they reason, can be absolutely certain that their conclusions have been derived free of the workings of habit, assumption, prejudice, cultural limitations or, for that matter, "intuition." There may be no pure intuition, but there is no pure reason either' (218).

The cultivation of perception, that is, the conscious 'expansion' of sense literacy, has long been associated with spiritual practice which includes the conscious deprivation of particular senses in order to heighten others (meditation and retreat, for example). Certain spiritual practices have been conceptualised and presented as more closely associated with supranatural perception than others, of which shamanism is an example (the category of shamanism is not without controversy, but these issues are not of prime concern herein. For a concise overview of the category formation and limitations see Ronald Hutton 2001). Indeed, Neil S. Price (2001) in *The Archaeology of Shamanism* considers the study of material culture pertaining to shamanic practices as 'an archaeology of altered states' (3). In the same volume, Damian Walter (2001) advocating for the use of the term 'altered perception' rather than the more usual terms applied to shamanic experience such as 'trance, ecstasy' and 'altered states of consciousness' argues:

> I suggest the notion of an *altered state of awareness* merely supports the idea that in a culturally recognised 'trance' state – however defined – the subject learns to identify and give precedence to different visual, aural, somatic and mental criteria, without necessarily implying that he or she becomes disassociated from his or her immediate surroundings, and without prioritising etic categories concerned with the truth or falsity of what is taking place. (112–13)

This is a significant point, as states of alternate perception have long been associated with forms of disembodiment, as evidenced in colloquial expressions used to denote someone in a state of reverie or contemplation being 'off with the fairies' or having their 'head in the clouds'. Arguing for a terminology that centralises 'alternate awareness' rather than consciousness foregrounds the individual's connection with lived reality and their capacity to manage multiple epistemologies – including those based on rational and empirical observations concurrently. To think of 'sixth senses' as expanded forms of awareness rather than different states of consciousness more readily allows for the knowledge they foreground to be normalised (and perhaps be not only the purview of the spiritual adept or designated seer), bringing the relational worldviews that underpin amuletic agency and efficacy into more conscious dialogue with empirical worldviews. Whether constructed in a secular or spiritual framework, material agency implicitly invokes other-than-empirical knowledges which the case studies in the following sections illustrate. Monitoring ingrained scholarly bias and prejudice towards such knowledge must necessarily be an aspect of scholarship that considers any such material agency.

Conclusion: Rude Amulets – A Disruptive Category

To conclude what has been the least material of all the sections herein, I wish to posit that if the category of 'amulet' as a particular type of material culture is to be maintained, then the types of amulets that are the focus of this study, that is, those with no invocational text or 'charm', be designated as 'rude amulets'. Although there are a myriad of meanings attached to the term 'rude', any association with 'uncivilised' is jettisoned in this usage – which is also in alignment with the repudiation of colonial mentalities – and the term is utilised here for three reasons: (i) an amulet's capacity – by virtue of its very identity as an amulet – to disrupt dominant discourses and worldviews founded in the prioritisation of empirically based knowledge; (ii) its association with the natural world and the 'wild'; (iii) its use as a term to denote 'robust' and 'vigorous' health (*OED* 2011). The latter term not only conveys what amulets are often created for, or directed towards, but also a sense of dynamic agency. Amulets are also 'rude' in their capacity to cheekily disrupt clear identification between prosaic and extra-ordinary objects, calling into focus our own predilection for the division.

This section sought to introduce amulets by providing an overview of their conceptualisation, as well as presenting both spiritual and secular accounts of material agency which furnish forms of logic for amuletic efficacy. It also sought to identify the broader concerns of scale, temporality, and inter-object relations which unfurl via the case studies in the following sections. Although, 'amulet' appears as a distinct class of material culture, their identification can be far from clear. This should be expected from objects whose very 'beingness' disrupts empirically based knowledges.

2 Enchanted Objects: Stone Amulets

> People may have invested certain stones with magical properties in a way that seems mere superstition to us, but their awe of what remains beyond the grasp of the human mind portrays, in the origins of such concepts at least, a proper humility.
>
> Beith, 2004:146

In the above quotation, the historian of local customs practised in the Highlands and Islands of Scotland, Mary Beith, frames the belief in other-than-human agencies of stones as a moral virtue. It is not mere superstition, but the ethical recognition of the limits of human knowledge and agency: 'a proper humility'. Although Beith does not make this determination within the bounds of contemporary theory, including 'vital material' or ontological turns, her point nonetheless imparts similar ethical ramifications. In seriously acknowledging that specific rocks, in particular circumstances, may have the capacity to effect protection and healing (Beith is particularly interested in healing traditions), the centrality of human agency and dominant epistemologies is both challenged and decentred. Although in contemporary mainstream discourse the practices discussed in this and following sections would more characteristically evoke credulity, nonetheless the attitude of epistemological humility, as Beith reminds us, remains requisite. This is not for the purposes of engendering any specific metaphysical or magical belief, but to enable respectful engagement with the material culture under consideration and the cultures which produced it.

The variety of stone amulets and the cultural diversity of their use far exceeds what can be captured within a single section, even within the limited geographical remit of the British Isles (with a dash of northern Europe). Nonetheless, taken as a particular type of amulet – what is being designated herein as a 'rude' amulet – these stones (some of which are actually fossil or bone) defy modern scientific attributes that designate the material as ontologically inert or *lifeless*. Long before the recent ontological turn in the academic humanities the agency of stone amulets featured in many cultures (and subcultures), particularly in relation to practices of healing and protection. In a specifically British context, for example, Tabitha Cadbury's (2015) survey of museum collections identified stone as the most common 'natural' material utilised as amulets (23). This section will consider selected examples of stone amulets to exemplify relations of correspondence (introduced in Section 1), and to articulate a framework which ascribes the potency of the stone to its relationship with a deity, metaphysical being, or spiritual force. This framework takes especial account of the temporal nature of the deity–matter relation under consideration; what I have termed previously trans-aniconism (Johnston, 2017).

In the ancient Mediterranean world, stone was attributed with a liveliness and interconnection to the physical and metaphysical worlds (variously conceived). It provided a direct link to its place of origin as well as existing within a network of ontological and symbolic relations with other material and spiritual phenomena. As Fabio Barry (2020) summarises in his work on the efficacy and symbolism associated with marble, the agency of stone was supported by the natural philosophy of the ancient world, for example, worldviews (including Egyptian and ancient Greek) in which substances were perceived to be comprised of all the elements: water, air, fire, earth (49). Indeed, it was not simply that these elements were compositionally requisite, but further, that each substance was placed within a specific set of relations: 'every mundane substance was a composite that had an affinity with one predominate element, an antipathy to another, and was neutral with respect to the remaining two' (Barry, 2020: 49). In addition, Barry (2020) argues, substances were not 'set', but were understood to have the capacity to change into another substance; they were always in-process, in an 'open-ended state of transformation' (49). Semi-precious stones were also attributed with a capacity for relations with a variety of phenomena, including human physiology, animal species, elements, and deities (63). This can be considered a form of ontological correspondence, a framework of belief in which a metaphysical substance or associative relation invisibly links phenomena of the material and celestial worlds in networks of invisible correspondences including sympathetic and antithetical relations. As I have reflected upon elsewhere, such correspondences provide the logic for the efficacy of material substances (including semi-precious stones) in esoteric traditions of magic and healing (for example, Marsilio Ficino who saw stones as 'divinely infused spiritus from the heavens' (Berns, 2015: 137–8)).

The interrelationship between stones and healing that Christopher Duffin (2013) terms 'geopharmaceuticals' is a significant part of geological cultural history. In Mediterranean and western contexts, the earliest documentary evidence or 'lithotherapeutical sources' (Duffin 2013: 7) are commonly identified as being produced in ancient Egypt, whilst their flourishing in western contexts is aligned with the emergence of early modern medical discourses that linked 'old magical principles' and 'new mechanic theories of matter' (Cummins, 2015: 166), and their influence into the eighteenth century (Duffin, Gardner-Thorpe, and Moody, 2018). Indeed, as demonstrated by Duffin, Gardner-Thorpe, and Moody's research, as well as that of Cummins (2015), the boundary lines between 'folk' or popular medicine and what was historically considered orthodox treatments is blurred well into the nineteenth century. This is also a point made by Beith in her discussion of the annotations found scribbled in the margins of the surviving medical manuscripts once owned by the learned medical families of the Scottish Highlands from the fourteenth to eighteenth centuries, especially Clan Meic-bethad (Beatons). These demonstrated that 'learned' medicine and its associated texts produced within the cultural centres of Europe, for example, Bologna, Padua, and Leiden, were practised in culturally specific ways and in combination with 'traditional methods and remedies' (Bannerman, 2015; Beith, 2004: 55). As indicated in the previous section, the theme of healing accompanies any consideration of amulets both directly and indirectly, as it is often an implicit aspect of an amulet's agency. Therefore, healing will remain a topic of relevance for this Element. As Duffin et al. (2017: n.p.) highlight in their volume abstract, 'magico-medicinal stones, some purportedly harvested from the bodies of fabulous animals, have ancient folklore roots and were worn as protective amulets and incorporated into medicines'. Fabulous animals await in the next section.

The skill of a craftsperson is also an acknowledged agency in amuletic efficacy, with Hugh Cheape and Alfred Gell noting the agential confluence of a specific stone's material properties in *relation* to the craftmanship of the human working that stone into any modified form (Cheape, 2009: 75; Gell, 1998: 23). This is a relationship conceived of as being mutually affecting. The 'lore' of stone relations, including 'invisible' ontological relations and networks of associative symbolism is extensive and culturally specific, nonetheless, it continues to this day, evidenced by spiritual and alternative health practices of crystal healing with weighty volumes like *Love Is In the Earth: A Kaleidoscope of Crystals* (Melody, 1998), that draw forward into contemporary times material associations developed in antiquity (often combining these with information gleaned from First Nations cultures, the nature of which calls into consideration issues of cultural appropriation).

Colour, shape, sheen, and find location are all elements engaged in the development and endurance of ontological and symbolic associations; for example, the 'magic gems' of late antiquity, semi-precious stones upon which magical formula and diagrams were inscribed (Spier, 2018: 142–4). The type of stone and its physical properties were of crucial importance to the gems' amuletic and healing efficacy (Mastrocinque, 2011). As Hall (2021) acknowledges in the context of medieval gem-based jewellery, the sensory aspects of stones, their texture, sheen, colour, and shape were thought to play a role in keeping demons occupied and bedazzled (492).

Translucent Relations: Rock Crystal Correspondences

To further exemplify other-than-human correspondences in stone amulets, this discussion will focus on one of the most renowned of amulet materials, rock crystal. Large, polished spheres are of course popularly associated with divination (the 'crystal' ball), whilst examples on a more modest scale, including in the form of jewellery, abound.

Generally associated with notions of purity and perfection, crystal spheres have accrued various interpretations, such as in depictions in Renaissance art, for example *Salvator Mundi*, (c. 1500) a painting of Christ attributed with debate about the extent of contribution to Leonardo da Vinci. The image depicts Christ holding in his open palm a clear crystal orb to symbolise 'the absolutely perfect, faultless and infinitely beautiful' nature of the divine kingdom (Haynes and Pissaro, 2019: 4). Haynes and Pissaro contend such spheres were considered to be made from 'solid light' and that early Christian iconography considered it as encapsulating 'the direct touch of God' (4–5).

The association of crystal orbs with holy and regal realms is also found in contexts other than specifically Christian art. Cheape notes that rock crystal spheres feature on the 'Sceptre of Honours of Scotland and in the Lord Treasurer's Mace' (considered the oldest regalia in Britain, their construction dates to the late fifteenth/early sixteenth century) and argues that the orbs are a feature of these national regalia because they were both viewed as markers of social status and as having an otherworldly agency, the belief that they 'bestowed reputed powers' (Cheape, 2009: 75; Royal Household, n.d.). The previous section has already noted that the placement of less-worked white quartz pebble deposits in the East Devon Pebblebed Heaths have been interpreted by Christopher Tilley (2020) in terms of spiritual power and aesthetic properties. These are properties that Cheape also attributes to the appeal of white quartz pebbles in Scottish cultures, noting that one found in Culbin Sands (Moray, Scotland) was 'mounted in copper bands', an act he interprets as designed to 'imitate the more spectacular amuletic crystals' (Cheape, 2009: 75). That is, the smaller crystal orbs banded with metal and suspended by a chain worn as jewellery and/or used in healing rituals, including being dipped in water which is then drunk (specific examples discussed below), were designed to mimic larger crystal spheres of more regal or institutional regalia.

Collections of vernacular knowledge strongly evidence a broad use of stones, including worked prehistoric lithics and semi-precious stones for healing and amuletic purposes in Scotland (Campbell, 2008 [1900]; Cheape, 2009) and according to Cheape (2009) this is a result of the influence of particularly Christian lapidaries which outlined the amuletic qualities of specific stones (75). He notes further that such lapidaries were a 'recognisable element of medieval *Materia Medica*' that had 'wider prominence as curative and protective devices in the period approximately between the fourteenth and seventeenth centuries' (Cheape, 2009: 75). Such analysis demonstrates that the healing and other amuletic qualities of stone were not relegated to the foothills of obscure folklore, but remained a discourse amongst many others in medical practice during these periods.

This amalgamation of different knowledge traditions is further demonstrated by Beith's summary of the use of rock crystal in the Highlands and Islands.

She traces both its use as a burning lens in sacrificial offerings, and its application in treating kidney disease to Orphic literature, whilst the utilisation of a crystal ball to hold 'the rays of the sun as medium for cauterising wounds' is ascribed to Pliny (Beith, 2004: 156). One of Beith's sources is G. F. Black, a late-nineteenth-century assistant keeper at the Museum of Scotland. His interpretation of crystal balls continues to resonate in more contemporary scholarly interpretations.

> In various parts of Europe, and especially in England, balls of rock-crystal have been found . . . . Many of these balls when found were enclosed with narrow bands of metal, chiefly of silver, but sometimes of gold or bronze. Formerly these balls were considered by archaeologists to have been used for magical purposes, but the general opinion now is that they were worn on the person as ornaments. At a much later period, however, the use of crystal balls for magical purposes appears to have been *common* [*sic*] in England. In Scotland . . . with the exception of the superstitious practices associated with the balls described below, I have not been able to find any references to the use of crystal for magical purposes. (Black, 1892–1893: 435–7)

This quotation, set within an extensive discussion of 'Scottish Charms and Amulets', neatly illustrates several enduring conceptual frameworks that haunt the consideration of semi-precious stone amulets. The first pertains to seeking to classify the objects as *either* 'ornament' (e.g., jewellery) or amulet, and the second is the ascription of 'magical' associations with particular communities – in this case peoples of a particular national state. Indeed, the taint of 'magical thinking' cast upon the English in the above quotation, is extended in the later discussion of the aforementioned 'superstitious practices' to 'highlanders'. That is, the examples found within Scotland pertain to communities who were cast, by dominant narratives of the eighteenth and nineteenth centuries, as both particularly uncultured and unreasonable, being therefore susceptible to folk belief and denigrated for such, or, via a lens of spiritual romantic 'celticity', cast as a romanticised 'otherworldly' culture with inherent skills in divination and magical practices (Stroh, 2017).

The difficulty in identifying for certain whether a gem worn as jewellery had an amuletic function, or operated within purely secular regimes of meaning, is considerably tricky. Mark A. Hall's (2021) discussion of dress accessories in medieval Perthshire (Scotland) concisely illustrates the multiple ways in which jewellery and animal adornments (horse harnesses and spurs for example) can be viewed. Any interpretation, Hall (2021) argues, requires the 'fullest understanding of the supernatural implications of dress and its accessories', and this 'cannot be attempted without acknowledging wider manifestations of magic and belief in the daily environment' (470). Of especial note in regard to the examples discussed herein is Hall's point that these medieval traditions continued (albeit with some revision due to the Reformation) 'at least' into the nineteenth century (Hall, 2021: 470). This observation is validated by Beith's (2004) research on the 'traditional' practices of the Highlands and Islands discussed later in this section.

Jewellery, therefore, could be read as markers of social status whilst also functioning as devices for metaphysical protection. As Hall (2021) notes, these apotropaic functions enabled an increased 'confidence' in the wearer, in 'diverting the attention of demons and averting bad luck' (471). That is, a capacity to wear amuletic jewellery could be understood as resulting *from* social status – having the wealth/family lineage enabling ownership – as well as contributing *to* an individual's social status. Access to the supernatural could itself be understood as socially significant, as demonstrated by Hall's (2021) discussion of the Campbell's *clach bhuai*, 'powerful stone' – a crystal stone amulet utilised in healing rituals. This stone, he noted, 'helped them to control access to the supernatural' (486–7).

In her analysis of the traditional beliefs of the Scottish Highlands and Islands, Beith (2004) uncovers the same potential for simultaneous use of gems as protective charms, healing agents, and jewellery (156). On rock crystal balls (e.g., Figure 1), she shadows Black's claim that these were a particularly

Figure 1 Drawing of Clach Dearg or Stone Ardvorlich. Originally published in James Young Simpson's *Archæological Essays, volume 1*, edited by John Stuart (Edinburgh: Edmonston and Douglas, 1872).

English practice, and that 'the Gaels do not seem to have used them for this purpose', an unsurprising assertion given that Black is one of her documentary sources. Beith (2004) also identifies them as '*léigheagan*, healing objects' (156); so too does Cheape, who considers the crystals as possessing 'mystical and miraculous powers' derived from the stone's repute as a 'symbol of purity'. Cheape (2009) considers their spherical, globular form of especial note and records their use in the curing of humans and animals (75).

One such example would be the rock crystal ball suspended in a silver mount recorded by Beith (2004) to have been a valued possession of the Macdonnells of Keppoch (it reputedly emigrated with family members to Australia in the mid nineteenth century) (153). The agency of this crystal (known as the 'Keppoch stone') for 'healing all the ills of every suffering creature' was very specifically emplaced, requiring it to be immersed in waters at a local St Brigid's Well (*Tobar Brighde*), whilst a verbal recitation calling upon Brigid, the Apostles, the Virgin Mary, and angels was to be recited (Beith, 2004: 153). If reports of its removal from Scotland to Australia are true, one wonders what substitution was acceptable for activating its efficacy in a foreign land, or whether its potency was considered reduced once removed from Keppoch (albeit Keppoch is also a place in South Australia, the small town named after Keppoch in Argyll, Scotland).

In these accounts the rock crystal's potency is linked to its form and physical properties, especially its transparency and emplacement. This is a materiality that both enables symbolic association (especially that aligned with its capacity to refract light) but also, when used as a lens or light filter, the actual production of another physically observable agency – the direction of sunlight to generate fire. Therefore crystal (an earth element) is able to produce another element (fire). This process is a visible manifestation of its inherent power. The potential for such actions and transformation could be understood to reinforce ancient ideas that the recognised material elements of water, air, fire, and earth were each comprised to differing degrees of one other, as previously discussed. There is also an understanding of a transmissibility via another element, as exemplified by the Keppoch charm, with the medium of water giving a healing potency to the crystal.

Viewing Otherwise: Crystal Sight

The *Frojelkristallen*, Visby lens (Figure 2), is a small crystal ball ringed by elaborately worked scalloped silver bands. It crystalises (pun intended) another significant aspect of translucent stone spheres' particular material agency: their capacity to magnify or otherwise distort vision. The particularity of

Figure 2 Visby lenses, Gotland, Sweden. Dating from between the 11th and 12th centuries, discovered in 1999. Gotland Museum, photograph by Raymond Hejdström. Reproduced with permission Gotland Museum.

Frojelkristallen in this regard is discussed further below. Such a property makes any association with alternate perception and the attendant knowledges gleaned from such an epistemological resource more physiologically understandable (notwithstanding the function ascribed to holed stones for enabling 'second sight' (Johnston, 2017). One may look *into* a crystal ball to prophesise the future, but *through* the Visby lens to view 'this world' differently.

Frojelkristallen was amongst several quartz crystal lenses discovered in 1999 at Fröjel, a Viking-age harbour on the island of Gotland in the Baltic Sea. Their burial is considered a response to the threat of Danish raiders in the eleventh century (Schmidt, Wilms, and Lingelbach, 1999: 629). Some of the depositions, as depicted in Figure 2 were banded, providing the possibility for both suspension and for use as jewellery and amulet (Schmidt, Wilms, and Lingelbach, 1999: 624). The type of decoration found on the banding has been identified as typically Gotlandic of the period, however, the place of the crystals' manufacture is debated, with suggestions that they may have been produced within Byzantium, or somewhere in eastern Europe, after which it arrived in Gotland via Viking trade networks where it was then sold to a craftsperson (Schmidt, Wilms, and Lingelbach, 1999: 624, 629).

A particularly distinguishing features of these crystal spheres, and the very reason for their description as 'lenses', is that they have been identified as 'aspheric biconvex lenses' (Schmidt, Wilms, and Lingelbach, 1999: 629). That is, they could be used as a device for vision augmentation. Jay M. Enoch (2002) includes them in a survey of 'archaeological optics', noting that a subset of the lenses demonstrates 'remarkable control of spherical aberration ... in some ways they meet modern standards for image control' (641). This feature has resulted in the crystal spheres garnering considerable scientific interest, including by Olaf Schmidt, Karl-Heinz Wilms, and Bernd Lingelbach (1999), who argue in *Optometry and Vision Science* that the lenses were produced at a time when 'scientists' had only begun 'to explore the laws of light refraction' (624), albeit what the authors meant by the term 'scientists' in an eleventh–twelfth century context is not clear. Therefore, the lenses are viewed as technologically innovative optical instruments. Significantly, it cannot ever be known whether the magnification was a deliberate impetus for their creation, or whether it emerged as a result of seeking a spherical shape for symbolic, practical, and/or other cultural reasons (Schmidt, Wilms, and Lingelbach, 1999: 629). Nonetheless, Schmidt et. al. (1999: 629–30) highlight that the silver banding worked in concert with the crystal to produce 'distinct images of objects in front of the piece of jewellery' and that this was only possible if both the 'back side of the lens and the front side of the silver' were polished (629).

Therefore, with specific regard to the *Frojelkristallen* the relationship between metal and crystal was requisite for achieving visual augmentation. Schmidt, Wilms, and Lingelbach (1999) also note that during the proposed period of production, polishing required considerable labour, and that therefore the craftsperson knowingly aimed to produce the refraction and magnification, which they also argue resulted from the craftperson's desire to achieve a 'more interesting effect of the jewellery' (629). It is not clear from this analysis whether the proposed effect was desired for aesthetic or visual-distortion reasons, or even their mutual production. Further, Schmidt Wilms, and Lingelbach (1999) will not countenance that the maker necessarily had any 'detailed knowledge' on how crystal should be shaped to achieve visual magnification effects nor, in their opinion, the mathematical knowledge requisite for such purposeful design (629). Rather, they propose the effect was achieved via trial and error. Ultimately, the form of knowledge employed to construct the lenses is unknowable, but 'scientific'/mathematical capacity should not be summarily ruled out purely because of the Viking-period context of production (especially if the production site for the crystal is Byzantium, considering opportunities for trade encounters with medieval Islamic mathematics). It should also be noted in passing that the use of semi-precious stones, particularly lodestones, are thought to have been used for navigation by the Vikings (Gelsinger, 1970). However, there is no conjecture that the *Frojelkristallen* would have had any such role or purpose in that regard. That stone devices were used for navigation, however, does demonstrate a conceptualisation of the interconnected nature of stones and the broader world. The stones possessed a knowledge and/or existed in relations through which their behaviours and interconnections could be utilised to direct human behaviour and networks.

Frojelkristallen draws to the fore the possibility of concurrent physical and metaphysical properties directing an object's construction and use. Its base materiality – both stone and metal – each carrying their own practical and symbolic associations, are combined together to create a potent object. Unlike the engraved crystal sphere recovered from an Iron Age funerary deposit in Årslev (collection National Museum of Denmark), with its apparent amuletic function denoted by the palindrome inscription it bears, which is aligned with cults of Abrasax (Gnostic deity Abraxas) (National Museum of Denmark, n.d.). *Frojelkristallen* holds no specific dedication. Not least, one suspects, because such a marking would interrupt, or perhaps annul entirely, the visual augmentation produced by the lens. Looking through the crystal makes the world strange. This strangeness is not the alterity of an all-encompassing trance or enveloping dream state, or even a filmic-style vision of elsewhere gleaned in the depths of a divination ball, but the recognisable 'everyday' world made peculiar. How can we, over a thousand years subsequent, conceptualise how that difference was interpreted?

The short, truthful, but uninspiring answer is that we cannot ever know for sure how such a change in perspective was understood. Nor the degree to which the visual augmentation was considered extraordinary or prosaic; a consideration to be held uppermost in mind as the desire to explore more creative and speculative considerations takes hold. As I have noted elsewhere, the interrelationship of capacities for metaphysical styles of vision ('second sight') generated as the result of the possession of special rock amulets is well evidenced in the Scottish tales of the Brahan Seer (Henderson and Cowan, 2001; Johnston, 2017). This was a vision variously ascribed to the gifting of the stone by the fairies, and/or its potency formed via its gifting in reward for an act of charity to a stranger. In this narrative, the stone is given to the Seer's mother by the ghost of a Norwegian princess who was drowned at sea, as payment for her burial on land (Sutherland, 2009: 15). Its use could foretell the future or enable clear perception of the operations of the otherwise invisible activities of the fairy peoples. The stone involved was not crystal or semi-precious, and the gift of 'second sight' was a result of its specific materiality and the capacity to look through the whole at its centre. In considering the *Frojelkristallen*, could the refraction seen through the transparent crystal similarly be interpreted as viewing an otherworld? Was the causation of this visual change understood in purely physical or metaphysical terms, or both simultaneously?

Despite the ambiguity of the answers to such questions, crystal orbs, whether large devices of divination or small amulets, via their obvious capacity to alter visual perception do invoke epistemologies and modes of consciousness other than those that are understood in our world as regular forms of consciousness. Just as ritual practices requiring body–mind cultivation, for example, prayer and fasting, lead to 'altered' states of consciousness that are in turn interpreted as facilitating connection with the divine or metaphysical realms, so too, by the act of looking through the precious crystal an individual's perception is changed, heightened, concentrated, and/or made ambiguous. Such changes need not be assumed to be mere curiosity, but potentially furnish the ground of relational ontologies: elemental, physical, and metaphysical. Even the now-familiar experience of magnification could be understood to refigure an individual's relations with physical and metaphysical phenomena. The *Frojelkristallen*'s potency is also speed. It has the capacity to elicit an altered vision and the specific knowledge that experience brings, *quickly*, at a glance, not via a protracted period of concentration or meditation. As this final section explores, stone amulets are multi-temporal solids.

Temporality: Fast and Slow Amulets

Alongside consideration of the ways in which an amulet's material properties elicit observable and/or physical change – generating heat or distorting vision in the case of small crystal spheres – is the issue of the nature of their proposed connection to the source of otherworldly agency. That is, from what source their apotropaic or healing potency is thought to be derived and the temporal limits of that potency, for example, the two pebble amulets from St Adrian's Well (Figure 3). Stone is of special note in this regard, as emphasised by Beith (2004): 'while flesh and vegetation were corruptible, the smallest pebble, like the grandest rock, endured' (145). It is this capacity to endure through the dynamics of anthropocentric (if not geological) time that leads Beith (2004) to contend that stones 'transcend time' (145). It is in such a framework that the durability of stone would indeed be considered magical.

Yet, this durability is not the only efficacy requirement. As previously noted, the protection and cure amulets afford was believed to rely upon physical proximity. The stone amulet is worn on the body, held in the hand, sewn into clothing, or its agency transferred via another elemental medium, like water, which is in turn ingested (cf. Cadbury, 2015: 201). Physical contact matters, and the amulet's own physical behaviour in relation to its environment also mattered. Anna Ritchie's recording of Scottish 'cold stone' (natural pebble) customs demonstrates this clearly: 'Water into which such a pebble had been dipped was believed to have healing powers when given to cattle to drink; the pebble acted as an omen as well, for if it dried quickly the animal would recover

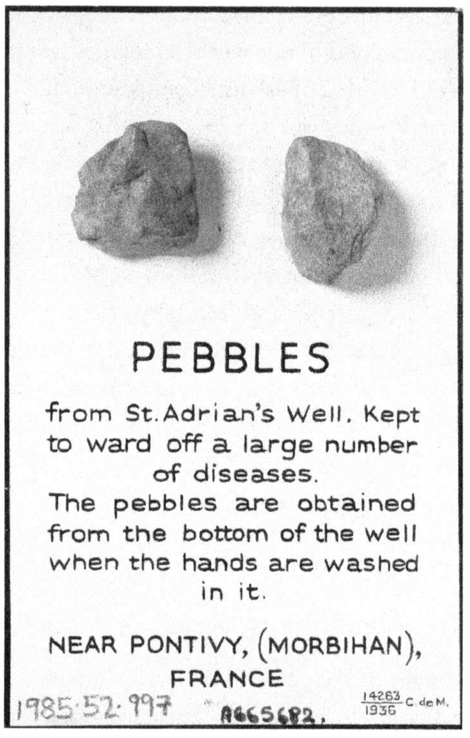

Figure 3 Amulet, two pebbles from St Adrian's Well, glued to a paper and glass mount. Pitt Rivers Museum. 1985.52.997. Copyright Pitt Rivers Museum, University of Oxford.

swiftly, and if it dried slowly the animal would make only a slow recovery' (Beith qtg. Ritchie, 2004: 151; Ritchie, 1974: 299). Beith (2004) recorded that just such a cold stone, an 'oval light-brown pebble', was previously owned by an Angus farmer in the 1870s who 'kept it in a small leather bag around his neck' (152), and is now in the collection of the National Museum of Antiquities of Scotland (NMA). Material culture of this type is catalogued by the Museum as 'charmstone', and currently the database lists over thirty such stones, several of which are on display, including a pebble of quartzite 'probably used as a charmstone' Many stones of the pebble variety are catalogued with the ubiquitous phrase 'probably used as a charmstone', denoting the lack of specific details in identificatory records, including vernacular use. However, some specificity is recorded, for example, a worked stone shaped into a figure of eight (M.HX 697) from Bothwell Castle in Lanarkshire, listed as a 'charmstone for piles' (NMS). One wonders whether the 'figure of eight' shape was crafted in semblance of buttocks. The procedure of its application is also not detailed.

As Ritchie's fieldwork attests, an amulet's healing efficacy could be embedded process, one that is operationalised by the transference of its power to another medium, for example, water. The behaviour of the stone itself, whether it dried fast or slowly, was interpreted as providing another form of knowledge, in this example, as a predication of the animal's recovery time. So too, an amulet's relationship with a specific deity can also be considered to be 'trans-aniconic', a term I have used to mean that an amulet may have an inconsistent and temporal relation with the source of its special power (Johnston, 2017: 456). It is not, simply, as is evoked by the term aniconic, that a non-representational material object is considered to presence a divinity or metaphysical being (even indirectly, for example lithics, considered to be 'elf shot' or 'elf bolt' (Campbell in Black, 2005: 223; Dowd, 2018: 451)), but rather, that amulets may be considered only temporary repositories of such agency, and/or that its efficacy is considered the result of both its relation (invisible or tangible) with a specific deity and its own inert material qualities (shape, colour, translucency, etc.). Most significantly, the term seeks to evidence that the stone amulets are a medium: 'an active (not passive) site of transitive exchange between human and other-than-human agencies' (Johnston, 2017: 456).

The liveliness of prehistoric stone artefacts, inclusive of flint arrowheads and monolithic structures like Irish ringforts has been emphasised by archaeologist Marion Dowd. She correctly discerns that such artefacts when interpreted from an archaeological point of view are 'seen as "inactive" and "dead"', as they relate to 'the distant past and now vanished societies' (Dowd, 2018: 453). In contrast, writing specifically about the prehistoric material culture of Ireland, Dowd (2018) highlights that: 'much of this same archaeological material was understood as evidence of a supernatural race of beings that coexisted with humans. That is, these artefacts and monuments were "active" and pertained to an existing (albeit supernatural) population' (453). This supernatural population, the *Sí*, lived invisible parallel lives to humans, enjoying whisky, Gaelic football, singing, and dancing whilst reputedly hating 'iron, fire, salt, urine and Christianity' (Dowd, 2018: 453). The latter substances were employed as deterrents in traditions that stretched to the Orkneys and Shetland, for example, an iron nail being placed above a newborn's crib to protect it from being stolen and replaced by a fairy changeling (Marwick, 1975).

In English, *Sí* are commonly referred to as 'fairies', although it is worth noting that they are not the overtly feminised and benign beings that emerged in literature and art of the Victorian era. The material culture that is linked to the lives of the *Sí*, and indeed forms connection points between their lives and that of humans, includes prehistoric stone objects that via their association with the *Sí* function as amulets. Examples of such objects include flint arrowheads, or 'fairy darts' from the Neolithic and Bronze Ages, which were perceived as 'both the cause and the cure of illness', and the magnificent prehistoric polished stone axes, objects often with striking colour and pattern, silky sheen, cold to the touch but weighty in the hand, which were understood to be 'thunderbolts that fell to earth during a lightning strike'; these objects were deemed able to protect the home (Dowd, 2018: 451). In her analysis Dowd (2018) stresses that these objects 'did not belong to long-gone cultures, but to the ever-present *sí*' (453). This draws our attention both to the way in which such artefacts are inherently multi-temporal, as noted previously, but also that the epistemological framework through which they are interpreted carries its own form of temporal delimitation. A multi-vocal approach to such material culture assists in enabling archaeological, historical, and vernacular knowledges with concurrent legitimacy, respecting not only the artefact's many lives, and the many interpretations it has gleaned, but also its enduring liveliness. Such objects are also trans-aniconic, potent 'places' of relation between metaphysical and physical beings.

It was not only worked stone artefacts that received monikers like fairy or elf dart, elf-shot, and so on, in vernacular Gaelic traditions, but also natural pebbles from Scotland of the type previously discussed. In consideration of these stones, Dowd (2018) summarising previous research undertaken on Irish vernacular traditions, argues strongly that there was no difference in perceived efficacy between the found pebbles and worked lithics, arrow, or axe heads, contending that they were all 'equally powerful supernatural items'. Indeed, she argues that 'natural pebbles' were more common in 'fairy assemblages': collections of potent items the majority of which are pebbles (457). Quartz crystals, including those worked into spheres are also a feature of *Sí*–human relations. They were employed as amulets to protect cattle and humans against disease and belonged not only to traditional healers but also to individual households, with some collections also recorded as being communally owned (Dowd, 2018: 458, 460).

Conclusion: Everyday Enchantment

To be 'enchanted' is to be touched (for some tainted) by the invisible, the metaphysical, the spiritual. In utilising the title 'enchanted objects', this section knowingly positioned its consideration of stone amulets in epistemological frameworks distinct from everyday 'common sense' or knowledges that result from empirical observation. However, the discussion has sought not only to directly explore examples of stone amulets and the cultural frameworks within which the material culture is, or has been, utilised, it also sought to gently trouble the epistemological binaries that hold the efficacy of stone amulets to the realm of 'alternative' (often feminised) knowledges. As the *Frojelkristallen* exemplified, a crystal orb's use could concurrently be both prosaic and otherworldly. Stone amulets had very practicable, everyday roles accorded to them even as their own liveliness set them apart from others of their type. As the physical locus of numerous agencies – both physical and metaphysical – they evidence the limits of human agency and recognition, if not perception, of other-than-human agencies. This is the reason that Beith, in the quotation that opened this section, designates those who acknowledged the stone's own agency (whether designated 'magical' or otherwise) as a mark of humility. They are small but powerful markers of the unknown, relational devices negotiating across time, place, and species. It is to the latter that the next section turns.

3 Enchanted Beings and Their Remains: Animal Amulets

This section will examine amulets comprised of animal matter, for example, feather, fur, bone, beak, claws and paws, and other types of 'pseudo-animal' materiality. The animals concerned exclude the human animal but include geological material considered to be from an animal species. In such cases this 'category' of amulet can exhibit a form of 'transpecies materiality', as they elide modern ontological boundaries between geological and biological matter.

The use of the term 'enchanted beings' in the section title has been selected for deliberate provocation rather than as a straightforward identifier, 'enchantment' being a term closely aligned with magical practice and/or alternate states of consciousness and knowledges. It certainly designates something other than modern scientific logic. However, in the context of this discussion of 'animal amulets', the politics of animal alterity sits at the heart of the amulets' efficacy. That is, it is their species-specific difference from the human that is most important. As numerous scholars have explicated, animals have been, by their positioning in dominant discourses, conceptualised as an unequal 'other' to the human, a positioning that has been crucial to the enablement of human exceptionalism. However, this section will not simply reproduce that binary. The term 'enchantment' is not employed to signal the animal as a mere handmaid to, or ingredient in, human magical practice. Magical practice itself has been aligned with historically devalued forms of (human) knowledge. Rather, 'enchantment' is employed to signal the animals' position of radical alterity. That is, the animal-other understood as entirely other to the human (but not of a lesser or inferior ontology). Pieces of their physical remains (real or 'pseudo') may be employed by humans for their own magical purpose, but the animal is more than a mere prop or tool. Its presence signifies a radical ontological difference; an alterity that is being operationalised in amuletic practice.

This alterity is encapsulated in diverse mythologies and symbolic attributions that have been developed by humans and attributed to animals. More significantly, and ethically viable in terms of power relations, are the varied forms of intersubjective relations between human and animal developed by First Nations' peoples. For example, animals which have been characterised as 'kin', or that understand the relation as one of mutual responsibility, and/or the animal as a 'co-teacher', in possession of their own specific and valuable knowledge which the human can learn, should the appropriate relationships be established. Referencing Neidjie's *Kakadu Man* to explain the concept, Joan McGregor (2018) describes kinship relations as ones in which 'humans are not separated or superior to nonhuman persons such as animals, plants or other natural elements, but are instead related to them' (119). As an embodied, lived relation it also accords with a change in epistemology, one that Tyson Yunkaporta (2019) describes as 'kinship-mind', an aptitude necessary to understand life as a 'sentient system that is observing itself' (170).

Such forms of relation are characterised by mutual validity; all life-forms, including the human, are valued equally (there is no hierarchy of 'being'), and/or the animal's knowledge is considered superior to that of the human. This can be especially the case regarding etiological knowledge. Therefore, the human can learn from animals by observation, for example. These are not relations that presuppose a human mastery or superiority over other species. As noted, these types of 'kin' relations are most commonly exemplified by reference to Indigenous cultures. This includes knowledges and worldviews that have been subjected to inappropriate appropriation through their inclusion and adaptation in western spiritual practices, for example in forms of contemporary shamanic practice. Clearly, usage of Indigenous knowledge and practice that is done without permission and out of context is a form of inappropriate cultural appropriation (see, for example, Donaldson, 2001). However, via concepts like 'contemporary animism' (Harvey, 2014) the vernacular and folkloric traditions of Europe have been presented as evidencing the residue of similar forms of human–animal relationships, especially in regard to contemporary pagan worldviews.

An animal's particular agency can also be understood to be present when it is read symbolically, depending upon the circumstances and context. For example, when the animal's presence (upon its own volition) is considered a portent either lucky or unlucky. A recent example is found in an article in *Bird Watching* magazine on the impacts of war on birdlife in Ukraine. It reported that the return of storks to locations of previous fighting was viewed as a good omen, with Oleg Dudkin explaining they have long been a 'magical symbol' associated with happiness, luck, good harvest, protection from disaster, and peace: 'Storks will always be amulet birds for Ukrainians, strengthening the hope for peace and the inevitable victory of spring over winter, and good over evil' (qtd in Winter, 2022: 32). This view of the stork is one which observes its activity in the landscape and extends these observations into understanding the relations of seasonal cycles and human behaviour. As this article also poignantly demonstrates, the storks' 'amuletic' qualities are not some arcane belief system but one that remains active in the lives of people faced with the terrible reality of war.

Given that the living animals could be accorded their own distinct (and to be respected) knowledges, attributes, and capacities to influence human lives both positively and negatively, it is little wonder that material from their bodies, feathers, paws, talons, and so on have been utilised as amulets. However, the manner of procurement would likely vary, for example, from a reverential removal of feathers from an already deceased bird to the targeted killing of a species to extract the required physiological feature. The killing itself can also be understood within a ritual framework, yet any such respectful observance should not be assumed, and indeed, in the case of animals that accrue negative connotations the intention would be quite the opposite. Animal amulets can also embody relations between different species with, for example, different body parts collected in an amulet pouch. In such cases, the amulet's efficacy can be understood as resulting from relations *between* the specific parts. Understanding the relevance and interactions of the pouches' different elements was the specialist knowledge of those who created them. The amulet is therefore a multiplicity of species (and elements) and a confluence of epistemologies and associations.

The previous section concluded with a consideration of stone amulets as multi-temporal solids. This section commences with an animal amulet that is trans-elemental as well trans-aniconic. Following this discussion, further examples will be considered alongside the diverse epistemologies which provide the logic of their selection, use, and efficacy. In the world of humans animals 'sit' at a confluence of epistemologies: symbolic, scientific, and mythic. Their presence in amuletic form encapsulates this multiplicity.

Chthonic Connections: Toad Stones and Mole Paws

The apotropaic agencies of geology extend beyond its earthy elemental realm in the form of toad, snake, snail, and otter stones, each of which are linked to the animals' physiology and in the case of toad, snake, and snail stones considered a *product* of their behaviour. These amulets have garnered solid academic attention (for example, Pymm, 2017). Although commonly forms of ophite, echinoid, or ammonite, they were also formed of glass beads (Iron Age) or even spindle whorls (Prehistoric) (Beith, 2004; Pymm, 2017, 175). These latter materials, like the varieties of stone, would have been sourced from or viewed as having emerged from the ground. Collectively, their genesis and ascription to animal species embed this material culture in a web of correspondences which detail alternate ontologies and epistemologies.

Identifying the earliest reference to 'snake stones' to c. seventh-century BCE Assyrian medical texts, Rachel Pymm (2017) provides an analysis of their presence, different types, and varying material composition across many cultures and continents from antiquity to modern times. This use, and the ways in which it is commonly interpreted, can be understood to straddle the fraught relationship between animal exploitation and veneration. On the one hand, clearly animal lives were exploited, species being killed or maimed to furnish the production of amulets. One cannot look at the mole foot amulet (Figure 5) without cringing remorse. However, it should be acknowledged that the animals' appeal for amuletic use was inclusive of a recognition of their *difference* to the human, their other-than-human agency and – at least in some cultural contexts – a respect for the knowledge and lifeways understood to be particularly held by them; not a 'generic' animal epistemology, but species-specific knowledge and experience.

Although Beith (2004) in her analysis of vernacular beliefs from the Scottish Highlands and Islands proclaims that: 'Few objects have had more nonsense written about them than the so-called serpent stones and beads', this is qualified by such 'nonsense' being deemed 'delightful' (156). Beith's attitude is unsurprising a within a modern empirically based worldview, however, the propensity to dismiss these beliefs as quaint also risks reinscribing dominant cultural beliefs and their colonial legacy on to past cultures. A more challenging if productive approach would enable such beliefs to remain present alongside modern analysis. Unsurprisingly, Beith (2004) traces the ontological claims of snakes producing the stones to Pliny and Druidic sources: 'In summer numerous snakes entwine and generate the beads from their saliva. According to the druids, Pliny continues, the hissing snakes then cast the beads into the air where they must be caught in a cloak before they touch the ground. . . . Such beliefs were still prevalent in the Highlands centuries later' (157). Beith's source was almost undoubtedly the Scottish folklorist John Gregorson Campbell (1836–1891) who, like his celebrated seventeenth-century predecessor Robert Kirk (author of *The Secret Commonwealth of Elves, Fauns and Fairies* (2008 [1933]), was a church minister and antiquarian and correspondent with Robert Boyle on the prevalence and practice of 'second sight' in Scotland (Hunter, 2001) noted in the previous section. Campbell records that the serpent stone or bead (*clach nathrach* or *glaine nathair*) was also 'a relic of druidism' and used to cure disease (Campbell in Black, 2005: 219). Similarly, Beith (2004) also reports that snail stones (*cnaipein seilcheig*) were hollow glass beads applied to heal sore eyes (158). One can understand a certain figural concordance being drawn between the form of snail shells and hollow glass beads. Akin to the proposed serpentine production of snake stones, Campbell reports that four or five snails were believed to come together in a 'mass' to collectively 'manufacture' a single stone of 'great virtue' (*clach shianaidh*) which protects its owner 'against all danger' (Campbell in Black, 2005: 221). So too, Pymm (2017) recounts that snakes were thought to make their stones in a variety of ways including the aforementioned saliva method, but also by repeated movement through an already-shed snakeskin or by creating it with their teeth (175). It is noteworthy that Pymm's (2017) analysis describes the accounts of snake stones (glass beads) as primarily being found in 'Scotland, Wales, and Cornwall' and that these were made most commonly from the seventeenth to the nineteenth century, corresponding to periods of increased interest and romanticisation of Celtic and Druidic cultures (175).

Other 'animal' stones were ascribed a more anatomical origin, for example the otter, frog, and toad stone, both of which are recorded as located in the animal's head. Campbell records beliefs on the island of Raasay in which the 'otter stone' was described as a 'jewel in its head' which when possessed by a human, made the person 'invulnerable and secured him [*sic*] good fortune' (John Gregorson Campbell in Black, 2005: 116; Johnston, 2017). So too, the 'frog stone' is located in the amphibian's head and described as a jewel of 'immense value' by Campbell, who also acknowledges that it is a type of fossil tooth (bufonite). In recounting its lore and reasoning for use, Campbell slips species between frog and toad to reference William Shakespeare's presentation of the toad as 'ugly and venomous' but 'wears a precious jewel in its head' (Campbell in Black, 2005: 221). Although not given by Campbell, the reference is from *As You Like It* 2.1.13–14 (Wilson, 2009: 22).

Recorded in the catalogue as a 'larger toadstone' of 'grey colour', the type of stone which forms the toad stone ring held in the Pitt Rivers Museum collection (Figure 4) is not identified. Its provenance is also uncertain beyond a European, possibly Italian, origin. The ring band is decorated with notched grooves. This ornamentation distinguishes it as valuable and demonstrates an example of concurrent amulet and jewellery discussed in Section 1. It is perhaps the mildly blotched surface of the stone that draws a visual reference to the appearance of toad skin which forms part of its material resonance with the species. Albeit, without more information about provenance and cultural context it is impossible to know why this particular stone was designated a toad stone of note.

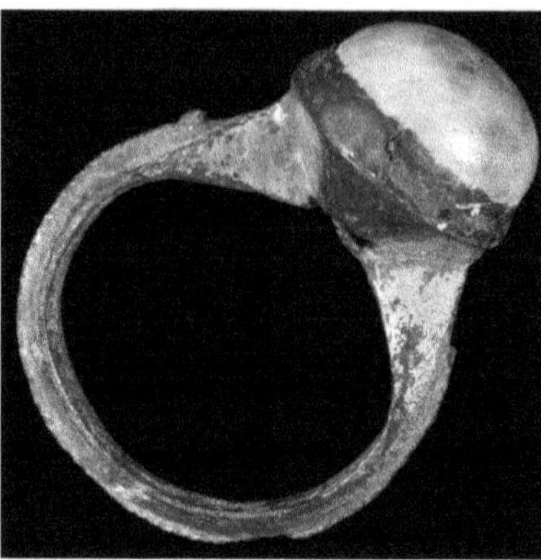

Figure 4 Gild-bronze ring set with a larger toad stone of grey colour. 1985.50.323. Pitt Rivers Museum. Copyright Pitt Rivers Museum, University of Oxford.

Unsurprisingly, 'stones' purportedly produced by, or found within, animals were not the only part of their anatomy considered amuletic. For example, in addition to possessing a valuable jewel, the 'king otter' (itself a beast of folklore, but also perhaps referencing the 'dog otter' – a term for male otters) was considered to have an enchanted pelt, described by Campbell as a 'skin of magic power' that kept 'misfortune' away from anywhere it was kept or anyone who wore it (Campbell in Black, 2005: 116; Johnston, 2017). Beliefs in the otherworldly protective capacities of pelts may inform their historic use in regal and formal military dress. Certainly, wearing animal skins to enact the transference of an other-than-human species' special qualities (as understood by humans, for example fierceness associated with bears), is well studied (e.g., McCracken, 2017). The latter also aligns with the role of dress in shamanic transformation (Posthumus, 2022: 189; Viestad, 2018: 154). A further factor directing the use of animal body parts as amulets are vernacular beliefs which considered the animals to be magical practitioners' 'familiars', species into which they can transform (yet another ontological slippage). As Dowd (2018) reports, the Irish *sí* were understood to be able to take the form of an animal, 'and hares in particular were often considered fairies in disguise' (453).

A connection to geology and the earth, particularly as a signifier of chthonic realms, is also evoked by the amulets formed of a mole's paw (Figure 5). The depicted examples, dated 1890–1910, are held in the Science Museum (London) collection, coming originally from well-known folklorist Edward Lovett's (1852–1933) amulet collection. The museum's catalogue records that the local belief associated with this amulet was the prevention of cramp

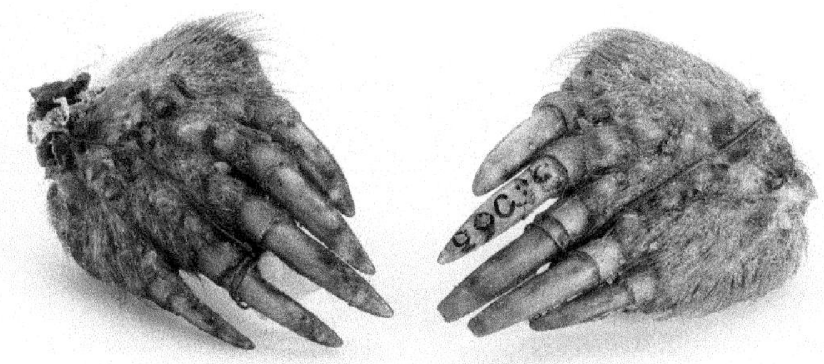

Figure 5 Mole's foot amulet. © Science Museum Group.

(Wellcome Collection, n.d.). The collector Lovell (1928, 15) recorded this association as a form of 'sympathetic magic' with the curving of the mole's front paws (used for digging) being associated with cramp, and therefore following the logic 'like cures like'; as an amulet the mole paw would cure cramp if 'carried in the pocket' (qtd in Hill, 2007: 78). 'Like cures like' is a foundational belief of homeopathy, a branch of alternate medicine that proposes that small amounts of that which cause the illness (indeed so small that in modern remedies they are not detected in contemporary chemical testing regimes), can be used to cure it. Examples are often of poisons or substances that cause allergic reactions (Shally-Jensen, 2019: 16–17). However, in the argument presented by Lovett, it is the shape of the mole's paw, its curvature, that is viewed as resulting from 'cramp' (or rheumatism).

The specific nature of the amulet's cultural (and emplaced) context is strongly evidenced by Lovett's reportage. If one was to consult Pliny the Elder's *Natural History* (*Natruralis Historia)* their recorded apotropaic qualities pertained to healing and divination. In a section castigating the 'Magi' (strictly a term denoting Persian priests, but more commonly used in Classical sources to reference those who utilised astrology and various types of divination often from or associated with 'foreign' cultures, for example, Egyptian, Chaldean), Pliny demonstrates their waywardness and 'fraud' by reference to a purported veneration of moles: 'they look upon the mole of all living creatures with the greatest of awe . . . to no creature do they attribute more supernatural properties' (Book XXX, VII (Jones, 1938: 291). Albeit these otherworldly insights and protections result from the killing or maiming of the mole: 'if anyone eats its heart, fresh and still beating, they promise powers of divination . . . a tooth extracted from a living mole and attached as an amulet, cures toothache' (Book XXX, VII). Yet moles' subterranean habits also align them further with chthonic realms and in particular treasures, as their burrowing (along with that of hares, rabbits, and badgers) has the potential to unearth buried or lost objects, coins, and lost jewellery for example, and including what we would now consider prehistoric artefacts, like glass beads.

Taking a 'new materialist' approach to considering the activity of amulets in the Wellcome collection (including Lovett's mole paw) and its exhibition in the history of medicine, Jude Hall claims their presence – even when being presented as precursors to modern medicine – undermines any simple 'narrative of evolution' regarding the development of medicine. Their materiality, find locations, and date-range of use (concurrent with the Wellcome museum's original display development) disrupts, Hall (2007) argues, any attempt to position amulets as purely something of the past, but rather that 'magic and modernity were closely interlinked' (68). Further, she considers their isolation in display vitrines as 'specimens', rather than denuding the objects of meaning, could be interpreted as reinforcing the magical agency of the various amulets, with the display cases working to contain their power (Hall, 2007: 68). Although outside the scope of this short study, taking other-than-human agency seriously will require scholars to consider the dynamics of material agency in museum spaces. This is a far from straightforward task, given the implicit alternative range of perception, epistemology, and worldview required.

Bone and Shell: Vegetal Transformations

In her survey of amulet collections in British Museums, Tabitha Cadbury (2015) notes that after stone, fossils (eighty-one), bone (seventy-seven), and shell (forty) are the most common materials used for amuletic construction (23). Figure 6 provides not only an example of this usage, created as it is from carved bone and two mother of pearl pieces, but also of another form on ontological slippage. In this case animal materiality (bone and shell) is transformed into plant matter (acorns) to produce the amulet. It is, however, not known what animal the bone is taken from (and the human animal cannot be excluded). This example is both of a material ontological slippage and of multiplicity. Although not every 'bead' is an acorn shape – some have the acorn ridging and funnel-like endings – the repetition of the miniature acorns is noteworthy. Information on provenance is scarce, with the records giving the location find as 'England/ London' and the detail that it was 'used as an amulet against lightning (Pitt Rivers Online catalogue). Cooper records that in Norse and Celtic traditions the acorn is 'a symbol of life and immortality, particularly associated with the deity Thor' (Cooper, 1979: 10). Thor is a well-known Norse deity associated with thunder and lightning (and generally throwing things) who is also directly

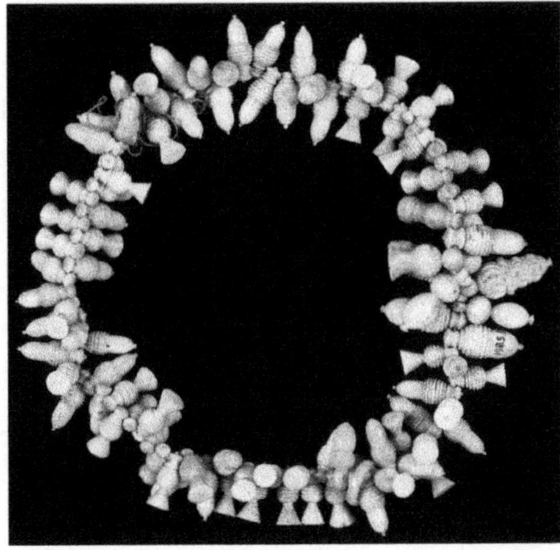

Figure 6 Necklet of bone pendants and two mother of pearl pendants, some acorn shaped. Used as an amulet against lightning. 1985.51.258. Pitt Rivers Museum. Copyright Pitt Rivers Museum, University of Oxford.

associated with 'Thor's hammer' (*Mjöllnir*) amulets often crafted from metal (Taggart, 2018: 174). The relation between the acorn and lightning is derived from the belief in the oak tree's longevity and its ability to withstand lightning strikes (Bintley, 2015: 84–5; Green, 1992: 152–3; Leroy et. al., 2020;). Acorns and oak leaves were also a popular motif in British medieval churches where its usage, especially in wood carving, is understood to incorporate pagan associations along with specifically biblical references (Fisher, 2017: 454). The Pitt Rivers Museum records several other examples of acorn amulets, that are either actual acorns or single acorns shaped from bone or metal. All these amulets are recorded as having been collected in England, and three are especially designated as an 'amulet against lightning' (Pitt Rivers Museum Database, n.d.: 1985.51.191).

The use of bone and shell in the 'necklet' is a notable feature (Figure 6). Given the associations with oak itself, one wonders why wood from that tree species was not used. Issues of scale and weight have presumably dictated the choice not to use actual acorns, with the translation of form into bone and mother of pearl a decision of both necessity and symbolism. Bone especially, would have been a durable and relatively lightweight material. It is also of potentially wide availability (depending upon whether a particular type was sought), whilst the few mother of pearl inclusions are a rarer material, of which its sheen and colour refraction could be understood to enhance its allure and amuletic potency.

Figure 6 is also distinguished by the plurality of 'acorns' that together form the amulet, rather than only a single acorn as found in the other examples from the Pitt Rivers collection. The multiplicity can be considered both an aesthetic choice, enabling the 'necklet' to function as jewellery as well as a symbolic choice, each rendition of the acorn shape repeating the protective power. The mysterious nature of the other 'bead' shape is not easily recognisable as any other part of an oak tree (catkin for example), and which to a certain extent, depicts half the acorn shape without the fully rounded form of the nut base. Its figuration remains ambiguous. This example has sought to continue to explore the ontological slippages that opened the section, but rather than stone posing as animal, in this case animal bone and shell poses as vegetation. In both examples material qualities and worldviews inform the selection of materials and form of the amulet. The final section turns to consider the issue of material multiplicity introduced by the plural bone acorns through a consideration of amulet pouches.

Magical Relations: Pouches and Amuletic Collections

Interpreting collections of animal remains as the accoutrements of magical practice, and by extension identifying human remains found beside them as a practitioner of magic, has been a feature of recent debate in the field of pre-Christian Norse religions. This particularly applies to the female burial at the Viking site of Fyrkat (Denmark) where amongst other distinguishing objects (possible 'magical staffs') were found owl pellets, the jaw of a suckling pig, and the herb henbane (Mitchell, 2020: 667; Price, 2019: 169). As Jan Bill (2016) contends, the attribution of apotropaic functions to burial deposits is premised upon their relation to worldly use as documented in historical sources (142). Bill's focus, however, undertaken via an analysis of the Norwegian Oseberg ship burial (834 CE), is to extend amuletic constituents beyond material objects per se to encompass ritual actions. Of note in this context is not only the investigation of apotropaic magic but also Bill's (2016) interpretation of a series of carved wooden animal heads and bells found in relation to one another within the deposition: 'In the case of the Oseberg find the combination of very different objects was particularly clear and surprising, and their contexts extraordinarily specific', arguing further that 'traditional archaeological publication practices, with its emphasis on types and categories rather than contexts, may hide rather than reveal signs of magic rituals' (152). Whilst figuration per se is beyond the remit of this Element's focus on 'rude' amulets (despite a slightly wayward step to consider bone acorns), Bill's conjecture of the potential apotropaic nature of Viking Age art accords with other such arguments pertaining to the agency of design and image, including those of Alfred Gell (1998) which have been applied to a wide variety of ancient images and archaeological sources (e.g., Garrow and Gosden, 2012; Manley, 2007), and especially Lotte Hedeager's (2011) ascription of an amuletic function to gold bracteate. Although Bill's arguments about the magical function of the Oseberg carved animal heads is beyond the remit of this Element, it has been briefly featured for two significant reasons: (i) it exemplifies the rich and significant relations between animals and humans and the way in which the animals' agency slips across materials; and (ii) an interpretation of apotropaic functionality as necessarily requiring relations between objects.

In specific regard to amuletic material culture, amulets formed from various 'parts' put in relation to one another can also be evidenced in the numerous references to bags and 'boxes' in Scandinavian sources (including saga literature and legal records), that have been identified as a form of amuletic material culture from the Viking era into the twentieth century (Taylor, 2014). However, the historical accuracy and representation of 'magic' in the Norse sagas (and the underlying Christian framework through which they were produced) warrants continued careful consideration (Dubois, 2013). Ruth L. Taylor's research on 'deviant' burials in Viking Age Scandinavia cites a viewing by folk studies scholar and museum curator Carl-Herman Tillhagen (1906–2002) of an amuletic bag in the mid twentieth century which contained 'the ashes of a snake, a shroud pin, a vertebra, the tooth of a corpse, a coffin nail, a pair of batwings, a four-leafed clover, a five-leafed clover and an old man's finger', although the specific use for this collection of materials was not given (Tillhagen qtd in Taylor, 2014: 121). Another collective amulet utilising various animal parts is recorded by John Gregorson Campbell who states that amongst the traditions of the Highlands and Islands of Scotland it was proposed that 'there should be placed below the foundation of every house a cat's claws, a man's nails and a cow's hoof, and silver under the door post. These will provide omens of luck to attend the house' (Campbell in Black, 2005: 126).

Underpinning the selection of any such collection of materials are logics of association whether they be literal, symbolic, metaphysical (including invisible correspondent relations) particular to the culture (and including material from other cultures deemed 'potent', because of its cultural difference, for example see scholarship on the representation of the Sami in Norse traditions, Debois, 1999). In other cultural contexts the archaeology of shamanism seeks to read the material remains of singular and individual animals as amulets, for example, in Siberia and Central Asia: 'zoomorphic and anthropomorphic amulets, certain bones of fish and birds and assemblages of small sticks have all been interpreted as items of shamanic equipment' (Devlet, 2001: 51).

Where brought together, these materials act in concert, in much the same way that a ritual can be understood to comprise gesture, speech, music, performance, costume, place, and particular human and other-than-human actants, etc.; all elements being essential and all working together to produce the desired outcome. Amulet bags, pouches, and collections demonstrate that amulets *are* material relations, and that the relations between substances are key to their alterity and efficacy.

Conclusion: Returning to Earth – Deposition and Transformation

The amulet types and examples discussed in this section were selected to evidence the unstable ontology of their materiality, and to demonstrate the way in which a toad stone or bone acorn, or even a mole's foot can elide modern scientific categorisation and epistemological boundaries. In addition, with regard to toad, snake, snail, and otter stones the very alterity of these species is demonstrated by their attributed capacity to *create* the amulet stones. More usually considered as prosaic and 'common' species when viewed from a 'magical' perspective, these animals are wizards, the creators of powerful apotropaic materials which, significantly, are considered of benefit to the human. Therefore, these are no mere animals or lesser beings; they produce geology, mine the earth's treasures, commune with spirits, and protect humans.

The category of 'animal amulets' is far from cohesive, indeed, many of the examples mentioned in this short discussion have been used because they problematise the category ascription. Their material form denotes the capacity of amulets to transform and to enact trans-species slippages. The use of animal parts from different species (including the human) to form an amulet via their relations is also a reminder to disrupt an often-assumed view of amulets as singular objects. Even amulets of a central and singular materiality, like the toad stone ring, are never entirely solitary, their potency being inextricably formed via physical and metaphysical relations. These relations are crucial to their functionality and form part of their subtle materiality.

In his work *Physical Evidence for Ritual Acts, Sorcery and Witchcraft in Christian Britain: A Feeling for Magic*, Ronald Hutton gives sustained attention to the so-called 'witches pits' finds from west Cornwall uncovered in excavations led by Jacqui Wood (Hutton, 2015: 4–5). As Hutton recounts, the thirty-five pits 'had each been carefully lined with a swan's pelt, and contained between them more swan's skins, along with magpies, eggs of a variety of birds, birds' claws, quartz pebbles, human hair, fingernails and part of an iron cauldron' (4). The swan's pelts were dated to c. 1640. Whilst Hutton (2015) acknowledges Wood's interpretation of the pits as 'evidence of a pagan fertility cult carried on by witches' without dismissing this, and indeed commending her bravery in publicly acknowledging such a possibility he, offers an alternate interpretation, one he considers 'less sensational'. He argues the deposits could have been 'intended to secure protection or good fortune' (5). That is, they were a form of ritual deposit, and whilst it is not his terminology, Hutton's proposition can be considered as viewing the pits as 'ground amulets'. It is this relation to the earth to which the next section turns.

4 Enchanted Places: Landscape Amulets

On 9 June 2022, Kari Paul (2022, n.p.) reported in the *Guardian* that New York's mayor Eric Adams believed that the city's 'unique vibe' was due to it being built upon a 'store of rare gems and stones'. Interviewing a crystal expert, Andrew Pacholyk, Paul (2022: n.p.) confirms that the city is built upon the Manhattan schist, a unique bedrock that contains many mineral varieties including 'quartz, kyanite, and dumortierite' and that for those attuned to the stones, their 'special energies' can be felt more directly in areas of exposed rock. Contained in this short piece of journalism are two forms of amuletic materiality foundational to Adam's belief (if Paul's report is correct) in the physical and metaphysical power of crystals. The first is that which is most comfortably akin to amuletic material as previously discussed herein: semi-precious stones employed as personal amulets for protection and personal 'healing'. The evidence presented by Paul (2022: n.p.) is Adam's wearing of 'energy stone bracelets', with the article providing analysis of the various meaning and properties attributed to each stone. Nonetheless, the source of these stones is unknown, and workers' rights and the environmental damage caused by their mining makes for understandable criticism (McClure, 2019; Souza et al., 2017; Thomas, 2010). The second type of amuletic agency is that ascribed to the geology of New York itself. Encompassing a much greater area, the bedrock stones are attributed as providing particular characteristics to the human settlement, to the *place*. This is not necessarily interpreted as protective agency, Adam's reported claim makes no reference to such a role, but rather, that the geology affected the characteristics of the settlement built upon it, its collective qualities, and agencies.

This final section turns to consider amulets as deeply embedded, expansive, and collective. Previous sections have explored smaller amulet forms, those that can be sequestered on the body or worn as jewellery as the forms historically and most commonly considered as amulets. This section wilfully plays with the category to put it in dialogue with the no-less 'troublesome' designations of 'ritual landscape' and 'sacred site'. 'Troublesome' in this context, as previously, is not a negative ascription, but rather denotes an assignation with much productive potential and the capacity to push on the limits of dominant classification systems. Therefore, places identified as 'enchanted' or that are in some other way perceived as special, are the focus; these are proposed as 'landscape amulets'. As noted when first introducing this term, 'landscape' is an extremely loaded word, embedded as it is within cultural, national, identity, and aesthetic discourses (to name a few) (Johnston, 2020, 2021). This section expands and develops my previous proposition and analysis, to consider broader areas identified as prehistoric ritual landscapes, with a case study of a geographically smaller formation, the late Neolithic/early Bronze Age set of standing stones, Mên-an-Tol (Cornwall, United Kingdom). In both cases, as with Adam's reported concept of New York, the geology has been interpreted as a distinguishing source of local character. The seen and the unseen are attributed an agential role.

Boundary Beliefs: Designating Ritual Landscapes

As far back as 1998, the term 'ritual landscape' was coming under increasing critical scrutiny (Robb, 1998). More recently, new excavations of ceremonial spaces previously considered devoid of 'domestic' settlement are revealing evidence of occupation at a much closer proximity (for example Durrington Walls near Stonehenge, United Kingdom). Indeed, the modern conceptual dualism between private–public, domestic–sacred space cannot be presumed to have relevance for the British late Neolithic and early Bronze Age organisation of space. So too, the modern concept of single-use dwelling ('house', 'barn', 'hall') and of discrete sacred space ('temple') should not be imported uncritically when considering the material remains of the distant past (Harding, 1991 qtd in Robb, 1998: 165; Johnston, 2021). In proposing the concept of 'landscape amulets' this section acknowledges the existing critiques of 'ritual landscape' including the highly salient concerns raised by John G. Robb: 'Does the modern concept critically depend on patterns of survival and visibility? One of the more compelling questions is the possibility that the modern perception of monument concentration, and territorial boundaries generally, is largely determined by unequal survival and visibility' (Robb, 1998: 165).

Therefore, it is not simply the vexed issues of determining where to set the boundary lines of the ritual landscape, that is, what is to be included and what excluded and the rationale for such, but also a recognition that those decisions are made with partial knowledge. The prehistoric landscapes that Robb is reflecting upon are necessarily incomplete, even when it comes to the most enduring of building materials, stone, to say nothing of the role potentially played by even more temporally fragile materials.

Therefore, in discussing any potential 'landscape amulet', the purpose is *not* to propose a definitive spatial designation or original use for the discussed location and its attendant material culture, but to consider how that site and its contents have been inscribed and reinscribed over time as a landscape amulet. As Robb also clearly identifies, the category of 'ritual landscape' has been adopted and deployed by many different groups, and as such challenges many dominant narratives, including 'notions of a single, national, and unproblematic prehistoric heritage' (Robb, 1998: 171). Most certainly, the plural epistemologies often summarily dismissed or ridiculed within orthodox archaeological discourse that are utilised in understanding the designated ritual landscapes by broader audiences including spiritual, intuitive, and agential interpretations, are also engendered by the designation of ritual landscape. A further factor to be considered, as highlighted by Robb's analysis of previous archaeological theory, is Harding's (1991) point that proposed ritual landscapes were not necessarily viewed the same way or had similar purposes to one another: 'groups of sites could play different ideological roles depending on where they are found' (149, qtd in Robb, 1998: 165).

In Robb's (1998) analysis there are two usages of 'ritual landscape': one utilised within the discipline of archaeology to reference a 'concentration of ritual monuments', and the other is the way in which the term has been employed outside of the discipline, for example, by heritage organisations and spiritual groups whose discourses may include a mystical interpretation to similarly broad landscape areas (166). In Robb's analysis, the move of the terminology 'ritual landscape' outside of disciplinary boundaries allows for spiritual agencies to creep in. To illustrate the limitations of 'ritual landscape' as an interpretive lens, Robb develops a case study of the West Penwith area of Cornwall, a place renowned for its late Neolithic/early Bronze Age stone monuments. The discussion of a landscape amulet developed in this section is also focused on a site found within West Penwith, Mên-an-Tol. As his analysis interrogates, factors that contribute to a romantic aesthetic of the ritual landscape, including the particular appeal of monuments located in undeveloped or barren areas, Robb (1998) draws attention to the contemporary ritual use of the site (169). The West Penwith area, whatever the intersubjective relations previous peoples developed with it, is an active site of contemporary ritual in which the prehistoric monuments play a significant role. As the next section will elaborate, this focal role is that of a landscape amulet.

Mên-an-Tol

> I crawled from east to west through the ring-like stone set on edge in the centre of this monument [Mên-an-Tol] as a cure for rheumatism and was disappointed with the result, not knowing that in order to be effective the rite should be performed in a state of nudity.
>
> (Colquhoun, 2016 [1957]: 62)

It is both delightful, but also unsurprising, to find that archaeologist Christopher Tilley (2010) gave the opening quotation in his section 'Supernatural Places in West Penwith' (a revised version of an article published in 2001) to the eighteenth-century antiquarian William Borlase (1696–1772). Unsurprising, because of Tilley's commitment to, and significant development of, phenomenological and sensory approaches to archaeological practice. The quotation selected by Tilley is one in which Borlase expounds on the suitability by virtue of the 'grandeur' of Cornish rocks to be worshipped as 'Deities' by those people 'addicted' to 'worshipping rocks' (Borlase qtd in Tilley, 2010: 427). Borlase is well known as a polymath with a particular penchant for geology and identifying what he considered to be the remains of ancient Druidic ritual in the Cornish landscape. He is a figure that quite rightly should be evoked herein, bringing together proto-modern archaeological field-working methods (Naylor, 2003) and an ideological fixation, shared by many 'gentleman-scholars' (often clergy) of his time on the archaeological remains of the ancient peoples of Britain. Indeed, according to author Philip Marsden (2014), in 'the mid-eighteenth century, William Borlase had identified the idea we now know as "ritual landscape"' (255). Amongst those rock monuments is Mên-an-Tol.

Mên-an-Tol (Cornish, 'holed stone'), that which artist and occultist Ithall Colquhoun in the above quotation reports clambering through, is a monument comprising four granite stones: the notable holed stone (1.2 m wide × 1.1 m high × c. 28 cm width), two upright stones either side of it (height 1.2 m each) and a recumbent (fallen) stone below the western upright (Figure 7). It is situated in Madron, Penwith (Historic Cornwall, 2024; Tilley, 2010: 446). Historic Cornwall (2024) notes that the site may have previously been rearranged, therefore, at the very least the relations between each stone may not be as their original maker(s) intended (n.p.). Indeed, Tilley (2010) argues (following McNeil Cooke) that the holed stone was previously flat until water eroded away a circular basin at the centre (the hole) and thus its current position 'is a direct inversion of the original position of the stone in its natural state' (447). Highlighting the rarity of such stones, Tilley (2010) describes its vertical placement as having been 'curated in a uniquely meaningful way' (448). He interprets the form as a 'material metaphor for the setting and rising of the sun',

Figure 7 Drawing of Mên-an-Tol. Originally published in John Thomas Blight's *Churches of West Cornwall: with Notes of Antiquities of the District* (Oxford: Parker, 1885).

citing its alignment with 'important times of the year' as support for this reading (447). The stone monument for Tilley is primarily about relations to the landscape, providing a visual resonance or being in some way 'mimetically' related to it. Therefore, their positioning, Tilly argues, is strategically set apart from naturally occurring stone phenomena, like tors and stacks (for which Cornwall is renowned) to simultaneously avoid competition and to emphasise their role as a 'ceremonial foci'. Nonetheless, they are, Tilley (2010) contends, implicitly in relation with these naturally occurring formations: 'stone settings such as Mên-An-Tol all reference the visually most dramatic tors at a distance' (449).

Although there are very many interpretations of Mên-an-Tol and the West Penwith landscape, a number will be referenced herein, I have commenced with a presentation of Tilley's propositions to highlight a relational aspect that is core to the discussion of Mên-an-Tol as a landscape amulet: its simultaneous distinction from and connection to the broader landscape. In choosing to focus on Mên-an-Tol, rather than the broader ritual landscape of West Penwith, I could be considered as reproducing what Robb, following Lowenthal, would deem a 'marooned monument' approach (Robb, 1998: 171). However, a landscape amulet approach which takes into account plural ontologies and epistemologies necessarily views Mên-an-Tol as radically interrelated with its broader environment in visible and invisible ways. Just as Tilley proposes that its positioning is guided by a material dialogue with the landscape, so too an amuletic approach positions it as both distinct within and integral to that landscape. Mên-an-Tol exists within a network of visible and invisible complex agencies.

Embodied Participation: A Healing Amulet

Numerous vernacular discourses attest to Mên-an-Tol's healing properties. Although on a much larger scale to that of pocket-sized amulets, its efficacy is also understood to be reliant upon a relation to the physical body (albeit the duration of contact is considerably foreshortened); see, for example, Figure 8. These traditions have become part of the location's 'official' heritage discourse, with Historic Cornwall recounting several versions in public information about the site. This includes its role as a cure of rickets, in which children would be passed through the holed stone; as a substitute for the monarch's healing touch in the cure of 'scrofulous taint' (tuberculosis of the neck); and, as denoted by an alternative name, the 'Crick Stone' as a cure for back problems.

An account of the Cambrian Archaeological Societies' meeting in Cornwall, published in *The Royal Cornwall Gazette, Falmouth Packet and General Advertiser* on Friday, 5 September 1862, described a post-luncheon excursion

Figure 8 Mên-an-tol, neolithic stone hoop in Cornwall. Photograph. United Kingdom. Estimated to have been taken between 1920–30. Wellcome Collection. (Creative Commons Attribution 4.0 International).

to Mên-an-Tol at which the majority of attendees crawled through the circular stone hole, as the report continues:

> . . . as this stone possesses the remarkable virtue of curing all spinal diseases; and it was a matter of no small amusement to find that one of the archaeologists, who had declined to submit to the process, seemed at a later period of the day to have had the aches of the whole assembly transferred to him, as he walked down the hills with his hands at his back, as if in great pain and suffering. (Anon., 1862: 6)

In this rendering, the stone monument was not only credited with curing those who passed through its orb, but capable of transferring their suffering to another who was in physical proximity of the stones but who chose not to participate. The recounting of this anecdote appears a telling combination of gentle jest and respect for the monument's prowess in the matter. An earlier account in the local press recorded that the person seeking treatment has to pass 'through certain rites of initiation' as part of the healing process (Anon., 1888: 5). The legacy of Borlase's antiquarian-inspired histories infuse other perspectives on the source of Mên-an-Tol's healing agency, with *The Cornishman* reporting in 1914 that its 'magical curative powers' were 'conferred upon it by the Druid Priesthood' (Anon., 1914: 3).

As the latter account exemplifies, unlike the stone amulets considered in Section 2 and those that snuck, via ontological transmogrification, into Section 3, Mên-an-Tol's healing agencies are not derived from the network of associations and lore that culturally embed semi-precious stones or figural representation. Rather, its agencies are linked to the distinctive shape (hole) in one stone, their collective, intentional positioning in the landscape, and to those peoples, variously figured, including ancestors and Druids, who were considered to have created it.

Further, interpretations also emphasised the monument's relationality, not only to the 'natural' landscape as previously discussed but also to the celestial landscape. George J. Beesley, regarding correspondence that arose after his publication about Mên-an-Tol in *The Antiquary* (1914) reports that: 'Some correspondents try to associate the Mên-an-Tol with sun worship and phallic rites', both propositions Beesley (1915) dismisses after consulting with a 'well-known Italian antiquary in Rome' (387–8). In abeyance of this strong conviction, the focus for this discussion will be the stone settings' relational exchanges.

Veneration: Trans-aniconic Relations

Mên-an-Tol's status as a focal point in the landscape is inscribed not only by the antiquarian reports of its use for vernacular healing practices, but has been continually reinscribed by the monument's use in modern and contemporary times as a focal point for individual and collective spiritual practice. Such practice includes acts of individual veneration as well as organised group ritual. This engagement can be understood as fostering relations with metaphysical agencies, whether personalised as individual gods or spirits (variously conceptualised), including land spirits or a more diffused concept of spiritual energy, that is unbound from subjective identity. Although there is a diversity of beliefs and worldviews that furnish this use, it is common to discern an approach to the stone monument that is trans-aniconic. Its material relation to the metaphysical is 'set to work' by prescribed ritual and individual contact which draws the spirits in relation to the human via temporal proximity and engagement with its materiality.

The discussion of contemporary pagan engagement with ancient stone monuments as sites of ritual and religious heritage has flourished over recent years (Blain and Wallis, 2003, 2012; Wallis, 2003). This has led to lively debates concerning access rites, heritage conservation, and communication as well as more broadly popularising viewing sites as contemporary sacred sites. It has also led to debates about tradition and 'ownership' amongst contemporary spiritual groups. Ethan Doyle White (2014) has contributed to these debates by discussing modern Wiccan interpretations and use (as distinct from contemporary pagan) with a particular focus on the work of Gerald Gardner (1884–1964) who is routinely credited with founding modern Wicca. It is in Gardner's work that the gendered and sexualised reading of Mên-an-Tol, dismissed by Beesley in the early twentieth century, finds an avenue into contemporary practice. As White recounts in the *Meaning of Witchcraft* (1959) Gardner devotes a paragraph to Mên-an-Tol as it 'typified', along with Stonehenge, the 'male-and-female imagery of early religion' (Gardner qtd in White, 2014: 66). White (2014) argues that Gardner's reading of Mên-an-Tol and megaliths in general as concomitant with a sexual male and female dualism aligns with Gardner's own Wiccan religious beliefs (66). These stressed the equivalence of the God and Goddess (rather than the predominance of the Horned-God), with White observing that the 'duotheism' was a Gardnerian innovation and that the megaliths were utilised as important evidence in making the case, and further, that they 'fitted in with his belief that the ancient religions which evolved into the Witch-Cult were both duotheistic and fertility based' (White, 2014: 66). In such a view and following contemporary gender stereotypes, Mên-an-Tol's upright orthostats become the embodiment of the God, and that with the circular hole with the Goddess, the dual divine creative energies venerated by Wiccans. Akin to a multi-part amulet, the different elements of the monument were understood to work together. The gendered and/or sexualised reading of the monument emphasises its collective agency, and is distinct from the 'crick-stone' usage which focuses attention on the holed stone.

White's analysis of early Wiccan perceptions of megaliths, as not only 'symbols of pre-Christian religions' but also as 'alive' as 'sites with supernatural links that were worthy of being adopted as places of ritual', made Mên-an-Tol a place in which deities could be summoned and held (even temporarily) within its material form. These views that White (2014) summarises were also influenced by vernacular narratives that perceived such stone settings (particularly stone circles) as humans turned to stone, or with having their own volition and therefore capable of movement (72). For example, the 'Merry Maidens' near St Buryan, Cornwall, a late-Neolithic circle of nineteen stones, has the narrative of dancers turned to stone attached to it. Further, and as also identified by White (2014), contemporary discourses regarding earth energies, including the ley lines of Alfred Watkins and Starhawk's designation of stone circles as being 'reservoirs of power' for particular use in Goddess magic rituals, cohered in the megalith materiality as well (72, 74). The circular form was also believed to attract metaphysical beings like the *sí*, or fairyfolk, who in Irish tradition were strongly linked to the remains of medieval stone ringforts (Dowd, 2018: 454). Therefore, stone monuments such as Mên-an-Tol were not merely significant stone formations, or even temporary deity vessels, but collected and palpated with divine energy. Persons attuned to such energies were able to glean and partake of this metaphysical bounty. Both historically and in contemporary times they remain powerful markers of alternate perception and epistemology.

The inherent other-than-human agency of Cornwall's Neolithic and early Bronze Age stone monuments is captured by artist and esotericist Ithall Colquhoun (1906–88) in her text *The Living Stones: Cornwall* (1957). Her magical and artistic practice was deeply tied to the Cornish landscape, with foundational beliefs similar to those attributed to the New York mayor Adams regarding geological agency. For Colquhoun (2016 [1957]), the rocks 'give rise to the psychic life of the land', and each different type has a 'special personality dependent upon the age in which they were laid down' (57). In her worldview deep geological time aligned with ideas of spiritual evolution: 'West Penwith is granite, one of the oldest rocks, a byword for hardness, endurance, inflexibility. That is the fundamental fact about Cornwall's westernmost hundred, and, unless you like granite, you will not find happiness there' (57).

But it was not just the geological foundation of the landscape that worked energetically with its inhabitants. Those rocks drawn into formation by ancient human hands were 'repositories still of ancient power, are the living stones' (58). Cognisant of vernacular traditions, Colquhoun renders the stones as not only lively, they can 'whisper', 'dance', 'play on pip or fiddle', 'tremble at cockcrow', 'eat and drink', as well as 'march as an army', and were also at the very heart of the region's essence and identity: 'these unhewn slabs of granite hold the secret of the country's inner life' (58). The other-than-human agency Colquhoun attributed to the standing stones was no benign force, but quixotic and self-determined. Recounting an initially unsuccessful search for the 'Ring and Thimble' monument (Lamorna area) she proclaims: 'antiquities are often coy and will not show themselves to the impatient' (63). So too, they formed part of a 'spectral geography' (Matless, 2008), that is, an alignment of ghosts and stone also featured in the county, with the latter also understood as being far from benign agencies (Trower, 2015: 164). This connection also highlights, as Shelley Trower (2015) argues, that there is a 'striking' relation between the durability of the stone and ghosts' capacity to transcend the mortal world (18). This is a concurrent ephemerality and durability that *grounds* the spirits, akin to the way in which an amulet holds and directs its protective and apotropaic agencies.

Not only were the stone monuments sites for ritual and magic for Colquhoun (as the previous quotation attests), so too her artwork was more than a mere representation of the standing stones. For example, her watercolour paintings of Mên-an-Tol, enabled – via a belief in shared metaphysical and ontological materiality – a relation between Colquhoun and the location's spiritual forces, its genus loci (Hale, 2020: 125; Johnston, 2021). The other-than-human agency that was amassed at Mên-an-Tol and activated for human purposes via ritual was also understood by Colquhoun to be transferrable to other media. In this sense Mên-an-Tol as a landscape amulet transferred its agencies not only to human bodies but also the creations of those bodies, the humans themselves becoming mediators.

In all these accounts of larger orthostats *in situ* since prehistory or placed anew, the stones were part of a trans-aniconic network of belief in which stone objects denoted a metaphysical presence. Further, these material objects *mediated* that presence in the lives of the local communities, manifesting in the belief of the transference of the metaphysical agency from the object to a human; for example, in healing ritual and in the perpetuation of spiritual agency at specific locations. In addition to healing, the sites were also associated with the development of extra-sensory perception for select individuals.

Stone Epistemology: Extra-Sensory Engagement

Attendant to the previous discussion of the use of Mên-an-Tol in particular, and ancient stone monuments in general for ritual practice, are not only beliefs regarding their power and potency or their mythic and metaphysical origins, but also links to specific types of knowledge and perceptive skills understood as required for and/or resulting from successful ritual. For example, in its overview of local custom associated with Mên-an-Tol, Historic Cornwall (2024) records the site's use as an augury to answer questions or foretell the future. This is achieved by placing 'two brass pins laid crosswise on top of the stone' which would then move of their own volition and 'independently' in response to a question (n.p.). Mên-an-Tol was not only a site for healing, a conductor of spiritual energy, or a dwelling place for spirits, it was also a knowledgeable agent, a site for the production of other-than-human knowledge.

Vicki Cummings and Colin Richards (2021), in a discussion of dolmen stone monuments (from the early Neolithic period, therefore proposed as pre-dating Mên-an-Tol) embrace terminology and concepts that would have been derided by their discipline ten years ago (and remain castigated by some). Embracing concepts of agential materiality (following Barad, Gell, Bennett, Gosden, etc.) they identify dolmens as 'being within the realm of the magical and extraordinary' (91). Their reading interprets both the technologies involved in creating the monuments, especially the raising of the enormous capstones, and also the way the stones are dressed (pecking and rock art) as 'magical'. In considering examples found within Cornwall in relation to the natural landscapes of tors, Cummings and Richards (2021) designate such phenomena as 'wonder-places'. These 'places of extraordinary and ambiguous physical qualities provoke a degree of ontological uncertainty and questions of alterity' (230). So too, in their conceptualisation, early Neolithic dolmens were created to encapsulate and generate wonder discourses of their own (228–30). Dolmens, they argue, are not conceived of as generators of benign enchantments, but were also displays of social power requisite for the establishment of new communal settlements (33, 221–46).

A potential corollary to wonder experiences is Terje Oestigaard's concept of the 'unnatural natural'. Developed in an exploration of the sensory archaeology of waterfalls, Oestigaard (2020) terms natural features that are 'ascribed with religious significance or divine powers' as the 'unnatural natural' 182). This term is not only reserved for large landscape areas, but according to Oestigaard may be applied for example to rocks, or unusually shaped trees (182). Significantly, Oestigaard observes that the 'unnatural natural' is also the 'supernatural' (82–183). Agential rocks utilised to form monuments in auspicious landscape areas can also be considered as forms of Oestigaard's 'unnatural natural', a grounded and materialised 'supernatural'.

The stones' capacity to enchant and evoke wonder should not only be understood as a conceptual experience, following Tilley's phenomenological approach and other more recent developments within sensory archaeology, because human engagement with materiality incorporates often concurrent, diverse types of experience. However, as the discussion of Mên-an-Tol has countenanced, agential concepts of materiality are inclusive of 'alternate' modes of perception as well. These are epistemologies that are 'othered' in dominant discourse but are routinely associated with communication with supernatural or metaphysical worlds and beings; for example, clairvoyance, clairsentience, and other so-called psychic modes of engagement. These knowledges are bound together with sensory engagement and conceptual wonder, processes that make observable 'everyday' perceptive capacities and their limits. The unfamiliar is uncomfortable because it makes strange our own bodily capacities to make sense of phenomena, and prohibits engagement with it in routine ways. Reading stone monuments as landscape amulets foregrounds this experience (in ways that more 'traditional' amulets may not) because of their scale, their capacity for full-body contact, and the alternate and multiple perceptive capacities that amuletic materiality invokes.

Conclusion: Communal Amulets

As trans-aniconic material, stone settings and monuments can be understood to exist in multi-temporal relations with other-than-human agencies, and further, to produce such agencies themselves. It also signals that the divine which the forms denote may be only temporally resident, and may indeed, not be attributable to any specific metaphysical identity, but rather be understood as an ontological constituent of the broader universe activated by ritual or gleaned by the use of sensory engagement and alternate forms of perception. It is, as is the case with all material culture deemed amuletic, a medium, an active site of exchange between other-than-human agencies, including the chthonic and the celestial, and the human (Johnston, 2017).

In this expanded context, structures like Mên-an-Tol can be considered landscape amulets: focal points of other-than-human agencies inherently (but invisibly) connected to whatever worlds are conceptualised by the community in which they are found. It is our 'response-ability' – that is, following Kelly Oliver (2001), our 'ability to respond' – in investigating such remains of the past to enable opportunities for these agencies and 'worlds' to come (back) into sight: an embodied, multi-sensory sight. Any such ambition necessarily requires entertaining, with play and reverence, uncomfortable ideas or experiences, including issues of stone agency, stone epistemology, and even the 'spiritual'. Indeed, if nothing else, the 'material agency' turn in humanities disciplines invites us to rethink the metaphysical and supernatural.

Evidence to support Mên-an-Tol being considered as an amulet is found in the site's vernacular heritage as recorded by Historic Cornwall (2024), 'The stones were also seen as a charm against witchcraft or ill-wishing' (n.p.). As noted in Section 1, the terms 'charm' and 'amulet' can often be used interchangeably. Mên-an-Tol can be interpreted as not only protective for an individual (especially those who wriggle through the holed-stone) but protective of the region: a communal amulet.

This proposition does not presuppose that all Neolithic stone monuments were attributed with the same amuletic functionality at the time of their creation, or in the reinterpretations over the years. Perhaps during the Neolithic period different types of monuments were ascribed different forms of amuletic agency. As has been evidenced herein, 'agency' and/or 'affect' are not universal neutral forces, but rather, a complex web containing its own diversity of characterisation. As landscape amulets, stone monuments were attributed their own agencies by the community, but were also sites where agency and affect were created and held in place by community engagement with the material; an engagement for which alternate perception and plural epistemologies were requisite.

Conclusion: Amulet Aesthetics

Dr Strange (2016) a film adaptation of the Marvel Comic superhero, presents a damaged neurosurgical genius trained by the 'Ancient One' (a Buddhist monk-styled sorcerer) to perceive and work with subtle energy. Acknowledging, but setting aside the orientalist and gendered stereotypes which abound, the film is noteworthy in this context for its depiction of the way in which subtle energy is used to form protective amulets. Projected from the palm of Dr Strange's hand – a traditional location for the transmission of reiki energy (Boräng, 2013: 22) – the filmmakers have visualised this energy as an orb or as geometric crystalline forms. These forms are then cast forth to form protective shields or to effect other types of energetic intervention. That is, they appear as stones of subtle matter. They are, quite simply, amulets whose constitution is subtle matter which is, within the filmic worldview, the universe's ontological principle. It has been harnessed and focused into concentrated form and then set to work.

So too, a practitioner of modern magic will designate their working space by 'casting a circle', defining in energetic, subtle matter a circle that is sometimes accompanied by a visual representation within which the ritual is to be performed (e.g., Pike, 2001: 7). It encloses the practitioner and keeps the invisible agencies they are utilising contained. This Element views the materiality of amulets as operating within a similarly prescribed spatial volume. From the smallest white quartz pebble to the grandest stone monument formations, all are a vessel in which, and by which, magical agency is concentrated, contained, and set to work.

This Element is entitled 'Amulets in Magical Practice', yet the reference to 'magical practice' is a gentle misnomer. As the examples of amulets discussed herein have attested, what constituted 'magical practice' was often part of everyday life, especially orientated to preserving life for the amulet users, for their families, and that of their livestock. To this extent, presenting amulets as specifically magical, with the term carrying all the modern connotation of the word, is inexact. As Cadbury notes in their survey of the material evidence for amulets in English culture:

> The amulets that ordinary people used seem to have been self-activated rather than requiring the powers of witches or cunning folk to render them effective. Men used everyday magic at least as often as women, while mass-produced artefacts were as potent as those that appear more appealingly 'authentic' to us today. (Cadbury, 2015: 205)

As noted at the close of the Introduction and hopefully demonstrated herein, amulets are as much mundane as they are magical and indeed, their very existence pushes on the boundaries of conceptualising magic as something distinct from, or counter to, the practices of everyday life and the skills of 'regular' people. As I have cited elsewhere (Johnston, 2017), Hugh Cheape (2009) distils this best when he writes of charms and amulets that 'they are, perhaps quintessentially, popular culture' (88).

Throughout this discussion, amulets have not been framed as material detritus of dodgy and/or long-defunct belief systems. Rather, they are approached as the enduring material distillation of some of the humanities' most crucial and contemporary questions regarding the limits of human agency, and exactly *how* any other-than-human agency, no matter its conceptual foundation, is to be figured and accounted for in scholarship. As this discussion has argued, amulets deeply resonate with relations of radical intersubjectivity and interdependence, and require the cultivation of an 'amulet aesthetics' which is derivative of what I have elsewhere proposed as an Esoteric Aesthetics (Johnston 2016, 2021). This is an aesthetics concerned with the apprehension of invisible, energetic relations and the perceptive skills required to do so. It is not necessary for users of amulets to understand nor perceive its material ontology and agency for it to be believed effective. Yet this agency and its alterity remain core to the designation 'amulet'.

Indeed, as Section 3 sought to explore, amulets not only slip across or make unstable ontological boundaries; they can also be a multiplicity. To use a term popular for Deleuzians' (and in the wake of 'new materialisms' taken up with renewed meaning in archaeology) they can be 'assemblages', but only in the sense articulated by Govier and Steel (2021). Eschewing analogies with 'collection' or 'gathering' of discrete objects, Govier and Steel (2021) focus on the 'dynamic' and 'open-ended becoming' of materiality (311). Amulets are a type of material culture in which that open-ended becoming is always-already in place. It is inherent in their very concurrent physical and metaphysical materiality. Therefore, an amulet's materiality is never stable, it is always in dialogue. Amulets have no inherent 'essence', but rather, are a locus or accretion of an activated agential productivity.

This Element has detailed how amulets can be singular, collective, and dispersed. They can be small in scale, of rude materiality, or the finest gem and jewellery production, or even formed from large stone monuments continually reinscribed by diverse ritual and multi-vocal interpretation. The amuletic qualities of our everyday materials live along and with us, whether consciously acknowledged and directed via magical intent or not. At the very least, this Element has striven to elucidate that amulets are not deviant materialities, but very *normal* and valued possessions set to work in average everyday lives. They are, above all, relational objects; setting the individual and community in dialogue with other-than-human agencies however conceptualised. Their remit is ever-present action and relation. 'Amulet' therefore is not so much a noun as a verb.

References

Asdal, K. (2003). The Problematic Nature of Nature: The Post-Constructivist Challenge to Environmental History. *History and Theory*, 42, 60–74.

Bannerman, J. (2015 (1998)). *The Beatons: A Medical Kindred in the Classical Gaelic Tradition*. Edinburgh: Birlinn.

Barad, K. (2007). *Meeting the Universe Halfway: Quantum Physics and the Entanglement of Matter and Meaning*. Durham: Duke University Press.

Barcan, R. (2009). Intuition and Reason in the New Age: A Cultural Study of Medical Clairvoyance. In D. Howes, ed., *The Sixth Sense Reader*. Oxford: Berg, pp. 209–32.

Barraclough, E. R. (2021). Trees, Woodlands, and Forests in Old Norse-Icelandic Culture. *Journal of English and Germanic Philology*, 120(3), 281–301.

Barry, F. (2020). *Painting in Stone: Architecture and the Poetics of Marble from Antiquity to the Enlightenment*. New Haven: Yale University Press.

Beesley, G. J. (1915). The Mên-an-Tol Revisited, *The Antiquary*, 11 October, pp. 386–89.

Beith, M. (2004). *Healing Threads: Traditional Medicines of the Highlands and Islands*. Edinburgh: Birlinn.

Bennett, J. (2010). *Vibrant Matter: A Political Ecology of Things*. Durham: Duke University Press.

Berns, A. D. (2015). *The Bible and Natural Philosophy in Renaissance Italy: Jewish and Christian Physicians in Search of Truth*. New York: Cambridge University Press.

Bill, J. (2016). Protecting Against the Dead? On the Possible Use of Apotropaic Magic in the Oseberg Burial. *Cambridge Archaeological Journal*, 26(1), 141–55.

Bintley, M. D. J. (2015). *Trees in the Religions of Early Medieval England*. Woodbridge: Boydell & Brewer.

Black, G. (1892–3). Scottish Charms and Amulets. *Proceedings of the Society of Antiquaries of Scotland*, 27, 433–526.

Black, R. (2005 (1902)). *The Gaelic Otherworld: John Gregorson Campbell's 'Superstitions of the Highlands and Islands of Scotland'* [1900] *and 'Witchcraft and the Second Sight in the Highlands and Islands'*. Edinburgh: Birlinn.

Blain, J. & Wallis, R. J. (2003). Sacred Sites, Contested Rites/Rights: Contemporary Pagan Engagements with the Past. *Journal of Material Culture*, 9(3), 237–61.

Blain, J. & Wallis, R. J. (2012). Negotiating Archaeology/Spirituality: Pagan Engagements with the Prehistoric Past in Britain. In K. Rountree, C. Morris & A. A. D. Peatfield, eds, *Archaeology of Spiritualities*. New York: Springer, pp. 47–68.

Boräng, K. K. (2013). *Principles of Reiki: What It Is, How It Works, and What It Can Do For You*. London: Singing Dragon, imprint of Jessica Kingsley.

Cadbury, T. (2015). Amulets: The Material Evidence. In R. Hutton, ed., *Physical Evidence for Ritual Acts, Sorcery and Witchcraft in Christian Britain: A Feeling for Magic*. London: Palgrave Macmillan, pp. 188–208.

The Cambrian Archaeological Society: Meeting in Cornwall. (1862). *The Royal Cornwall Gazette, Falmouth Packet and General Advertiser*. Friday, 5 September, p. 6.

Campbell, J. G. (2008 (1900)). *Superstitions of the Highlands and Islands*. Published as *The Gaelic Otherworld*, ed. R. Black. Edinburgh: Birlinn.

Cheape, H. (2009). From Natural to Supernatural: The Material Culture of Charms and Amulets. In L. Henderson, ed., *Fantastical Imaginations: The Supernatural in Scottish History and Culture*. Edinburgh: Birlinn, pp. 70–90.

Cipolla, C. N. (2018). Earth Flows and Lively Stone: What Difference Does 'Vibrant' Matter Make? *Archaeological Dialogues*, 25(1), 49–70.

Colquhoun, I. (2016 (1957)). *The Living Stones: Cornwall*. London: Peter Owen.

Cooper, A., Garrow, D. & Gibson, C. (2020). Spectrums of Depositional Practice in Later Prehistoric Britain and Beyond: Grave Goods, Hoards and Seposits 'In-Between'. *Archaeological Dialogues*, 27, 135–57.

Cooper, J. C. (1979). *An Illustrated Encyclopedia of Traditional Symbols*. London: Thames & Hudson.

Cornwall the Mysterious. (1914). *The Cornishman*. Thursday 5 March, p. 3.

Crellin, R. J., Cipolla, C. N., Montgomery, L. M., Harris, O. J. & Moore, S. V. (2020). *Archaeological Theory in Dialogue: Situating Relationality, Ontology, Posthumanism and Indigenous Paradigms*. Abingdon: Routledge.

Cummings, V. & Richards, C. (2021). *Monuments in the Making: Raising the Great Dolmens in the Early Neolithic Northern Europe*. Oxford: Windgather.

Cummins, A. (2015). Textual Evidence for the Material History of Amulets in Seventeenth-Century England. In R. Hutton, ed., *Physical Evidence for Ritual Acts, Sorcery and Witchcraft in Christian Britain: A Feeling for Magic*. London: Palgrave Macmillan, pp. 164–87.

Davies, O. & Houlbrook, C. (2021). *Building Magic: Ritual and Re-enchantment in Post-Medieval Structures*. London: Palgrave Macmillan.

Day, J. (2020). Sensory Approaches to the Aegean Bronze Age. In R. Skeates & J. Day, eds, *The Routledge Handbook of Sensory Archaeology*. London: Routledge, pp. 377–95.

Derrickson, S. (2016). *Dr Strange*. Film. 115 mins. Prod. Kevin Feige, Marvel Studios.

Devlet, E. (2001). Rock Art and the Material Culture of Siberian and Central Asian Shamanism. In N. Price, ed., *The Archaeology of Shamanism*. Abingdon: Routledge, pp. 43–55.

Donaldson, L. E. (2001). On Medicine Women and White Shame-ans: New Age Native Americanism and Commodity Fetishism as Pop Culture Feminism. In E. A. Castelli, ed., *Women, Gender, Religion: A Reader*. New York: Palgrave Macmillan, pp. 237–53.

Dowd, M. (2018). Bewitched by an Elf Dart: Fairy Archaeology, Folk Magic and Traditional Medicine in Ireland. *Cambridge Archaeological Journal*, 28(3), 451–73.

(2020). Darkness and Light in the Archaeological Past: Sensory Perspectives. In R. Skeates & J. Day, eds (2020). *The Routledge Handbook of Sensory Archaeology*. Abingdon : Routledge, pp. 193–209.

Dubois, T. A. (1999). *Nordic Religions in the Viking Age*. Philadelphia: University of Pennsylvania.

(2013). Magic and Witchcraft Historicized, Localized, and Ethnicized: A Response to Stephen Mitchell's *Witchcraft and Magic in the Nordic Middle Ages: Magic, Ritual, and Witchcraft*, 8(1), 82–9.

Duffin, C. J. (2013). Lithotherapeutical Research Courses from Antiquity to the Mid-Eighteenth Century. In C. J. Duffin, R. T. J. Moody, & C. Gardner-Thorpe (eds.). *A History of Geology and Medicine*. London: Geological Society, Special Publication, 375, pp. 7–14.

Duffin, C. J., Gardner-Thorpe, C. & Moody, R. (2018). *Geology and Medicine: Historical Connections*. London: Geological Society of London.

Easton, T. (2015). Spiritual Middens. In R. Hutton, ed., *Physical Evidence for Ritual Acts, Sorcery and Witchcraft in Christian Britain: A Feeling for Magic*. London: Palgrave Macmillan, pp. 147–63.

Eastop, D. (2015). Garments Concealed within Buildings: Following the Evidence. In R. Hutton, ed., *Physical Evidence for Ritual Acts, Sorcery and Witchcraft in Christian Britain: A Feeling for Magic*. London: Palgrave Macmillan, pp. 131–46.

Eckhardt, H. and Williams, C. (2018). The Sound of Magic? Bells in Roman Britain. *Britannia*, 49, 179–210.

Enoch, J. M. (2002). Archaeological Optics. In A. H. Guenther, ed., *International Trends in Applied Optics*. Bellingham: SPIE, pp. 629–66.

Evans, I., Manning, M. C. & Davies, O. (2015). The Wider Picture: Parallel Evidence in America and Australia. In R. Hutton, ed., *Physical Evidence for Ritual Acts, Sorcery and Witchcraft in Christian Britain: A Feeling for Magic*. London: Palgrave Macmillan, pp. 232–54.

Ficino, M. (1996 (1980; 1489)). *The Book of Life*, trans. C. Boer. Woodstock: Spring.

Fisher, C. (2017). Flowers and Plants: The Living Iconography. In C. Hourihane, ed., *The Routledge Companion to Medieval Iconography*. London: Routledge, pp. 453–64.

Freedberg, D. (1989). *The Power of Images: Studies in the History and Theory of Response*. Chicago: University of Chicago Press.

Gardeła, L. (2021). Interpreting the Arsenal of Armed Women. In L. Gardeła, ed., *Women and Weapons in the Viking World: Amazons of the North*. Oxford: Oxbow, pp. 81–116.

Garrow, D. & Gosden, C. (2012). *Technologies of Enchantment? Exploring Celtic Art: 400 BC to AD 100*. Oxford: Oxford University Press.

Gawain, S. (1978). *Creative Visualisation: Use the Power of Your Imagination to Create What You Want in Your Life*. New York: Bantam.

Gell, A. (1998). *Art and Agency: An Anthropological Theory*. Oxford: Clarendon Press.

Gelsinger, B. E. (1970). Lodestone and Sunstone in Medieval Iceland. *The Mariner's Mirror* 56(2), 219–26.

Govier, E. & Steel, L. (2021). Beyond the 'Thingification' of Worlds. Archaeology and the New Materialisms. *Journal of Material Culture*, 26(3), 298–317.

Green, G. (1992 (1989)). *Symbols and Image in Celtic Religious Art*. Abingdon: Routledge.

Hale, A. (2020). *Ithall Colquhoun: Genius of the Fern Loved Gully*. London: Strange Attractor.

Hall, M. A. (2021). Status, Magic and Belief: Exploring Identity through Dress Accessories and Other Amulets in Medieval Scotland: A Perthshire Case-Study. *Scottish Historical Review*, 100(3), 469–92.

Hanegraaff, W. (2012). *Esotericism and the Academy: Rejected Knowledge in Western Culture*. Cambridge: Cambridge University Press.

Haraway, D. (1991). *Simians, Cyborgs and Women: The Reinvention of Nature*. London: Free Association Books.

Harvey, G. (ed.) (2014). *The Handbook of Contemporary Animism*. Abingdon: Routledge.

Haynes, L. & Pissarro, J. (2019). *Crystals in Art: Ancient to Today*. Fayetteville: University of Arkansas Press.

Hedeager, L. (2011). *Iron Age Myth and Materiality: An Archaeology of Scandinavia. AD 400–1000*. London: Routledge.

Helms, M. W. (2004). Before the Dawn: Monks and the Night in Late Antique and Early Medieval Europe. *Anthropos*, 99(1), 177–91.

Henderson, L. and Cowan, E. J. (2007/2011 (2001)). *Scottish Fairy Belief.* Edinburgh: John Donald.

Hill, J. (2007). The Story of the Amulet: Locating the Enchantment of Collections. *Journal of Material Culture*, 12(1), 65–87.

Historic Cornwall. (2024). Men-An-Tol. Cornwall and Scilly Historic Environment Record. Cornwall Council. www.historic-cornwall.org.uk/a2m/bronze_age/stone_circle/men_an_tol/men_an_tol.htm.

Hoggard, B. (2015a). Concealed Animals. In R. Hutton, ed., *Physical Evidence for Ritual Acts, Sorcery and Witchcraft in Christian Britain: A Feeling for Magic*. London: Palgrave Macmillan, pp. 106–17.

(2015b). Witch Bottles: Their Contents, Contexts and Uses. In R. Hutton, ed., *Physical Evidence for Ritual Acts, Sorcery and Witchcraft in Christian Britain: A Feeling for Magic*. London: Palgrave Macmillan, pp. 91–105.

Howes, D. (ed.) (2009). *The Sixth Sense Reader.* Oxford: Berg.

Hukantaival, S. (2021). International Magic?: Finnish Folk Magic Objects in a European Context. *Temenos: Nordic Journal of Comparative Religion*, 57(2), 155–80.

Hunter, M. (2001). *The Occult Laboratory: Magic, Science, and Second Sight in Late Seventeenth-Century Scotland.* Woodbridge: Boydell.

Hutton, R. (2001). *Shamans: Siberian Spirituality and the Western Imagination*. London: Hambledon.

(2015). Introduction. In R. Hutton, ed., *Physical Evidence for Ritual Acts, Sorcery and Witchcraft in Christian Britain: A Feeling for Magic*. London: Palgrave Macmillan, pp. 1–14.

Johnston, J. (2008) *Angels of Desire: Esoteric Bodies, Aesthetics and Ethics*. London: Equinox.

(2010). Prolegomena to Considering Drawings of Spirit-Beings in Mandaean, Gnostic and Ancient Magical Texts. *ARAM*, 22, 573–82.

(2016). Enchanted Sight/Site: An Esoteric Aesthetics of Image and Experience. In P. Ingman, T. Utriainen, T. Hovi & M. Broo, eds, *The Relational Dynamics of Enchantment and Sacralization: Changing the Terms of the Religion Versus Secularity Debate*. Sheffield: Equinox, pp. 89–206.

(2016b). Slippery and Saucy Discourse: Grappling with the Intersection of 'Alternate Epistemologies' and Discourse Analysis. In F. Wijsen & K. von Stuckrad, eds, *Making Religion: Theory and Practice in the Discursive Study of Religion*. Leiden: Brill, pp. 74–96.

(2017). Stone-Agency: Sense, Sight and Magical Efficacy in Traditions of the Highlands and Islands of Scotland. *Religion*, 47(3), 445–58.

(2020). Rites, Runes and Maeshowe: Northern Landscapes and Lived Belief. In R. Ljosland, A. Sanmark and O. Plumb, eds, *What is North? Visualising, Representing and Imagining the North from the Viking Age to Modern Times*. Turnhout: Brepols, pp. 211–25.

(2021). *Stag and Stone: Religion, Archaeology and Esoteric Aesthetics*. Sheffield: Equinox.

(2021b). Painterly Desire: Ithell Colquhoun's Other-than-Human Art. In A. Hale, ed., *Essays on Women in Western Esotericism: Beyond Seeresses and Sea Priestesses.* Cham: Palgrave Macmillan, pp. 151–70.

(2022). Introduction. In J. Johnston & I. Gardner, eds, *Drawing Spirit: The Role of Images and Design in the Magical Practice of Late Antiquity.* Berlin: De Gruyter.

Jones, A. M. (2012). *Prehistoric Materialities: Becoming Material in Prehistoric Britain and Ireland.* Oxford: Oxford University Press.

(2017). Rock Art and Ontology. *Annual Review of Anthropology*, 46, 167–81.

Jones, W. H. S. (1938). *Pliny: Natural History With an English Translation in Ten Volumes.* Cambridge: Harvard University Press.

Kirk, R. (2008 (1933)). *The Secret Commonwealth of Elves, Fauns and Fairies*. Mineola: Dover.

Leroy T., Plomion C. & Kremer, A. (2020). Oak Symbolism in the Light of Genetics. *New Phytologist*, 226, 1012–17.

Lindstrøm, T. C. (2015). Agency 'In Itself': A Discussion of Inanimate, Animal and Human Agency. *Archaeological Dialogues*, 22(2), 207–38.

Lockhardt, M. (2010). *Subtle Energy Body: The Complete Guide*. Rochester: Inner Traditions.

Lovett, E. (1928). *Folk-Lore and Legend of the Surrey Hills and of the Sussex Downs and Forests*. Caterham: Caterham Printing Works.

MacCracken, P. (2017). *In the Skin of the Beast: Sovereignty and Animality in Medieval France*. Chicago: University of Chicago Press.

Maltby, M. (2017). From Bovid to Beaver: Mammal Exploitation in Medieval Northwest Russia. In U. Albarella, M. Rizzetto, H. Russ, K. Vickers & S. Viner-Daniels, eds, *The Oxford Handbook of Zooarchaeology.* Oxford: Oxford University Press, pp. 230–44.

Manley, J. (2007). Decoration and Demon Traps: The Meanings of Geometric Borders in Roman Mosaics. In C. Gosden, H. Hamerow, P.-d. Jersey & G. Lock, eds, *Communities and Connections: Essays in Honour of Barry Cunliffe*. Oxford: Oxford University Press, pp. 426–48.

Marsden, P. (2014). *Rising Ground: A Search for the Spirit of Place*. London: Granta.

Marwick, E. W. (1975). *The Folklore of Orkney and Shetland*. London: B. T. Batsford.

Matless, D. (2008). A Geography of Ghosts: The Spectral Landscapes of Mary Butts. *Cultural Geographies*, 15, 335–57.

Mastrocinque, A. (2011). The Colours of Magical Gems. In C. Entwistle & N. Adams, eds, *'Gems of Heaven:' Recent Research on Engraved Gemstones in Late Antiquity c.AD200–600*. London: The British Museum, pp. 62–8.

McClure, T. (2019). Dark Crystals: The Brutal Reality Behind a Booming Wellness Craze. *Guardian*. www.theguardian.com/lifeandstyle/2019/sep/17/healing-crystals-wellness-mining-madagascar.

McGregor, J. (2018). Towards a Philosophical Understanding of TEK and Ecofeminism. In M. K. Nelson & D. Shilling, eds, *Traditional Ecological Knowledge: Learning from Practices and Environmental Sustainability*. Cambridge: Cambridge University Press, pp. 109–28.

Melody. (1998). *Love Is in The Earth: A Kaleidoscope of Crystals*. Colorado: Earth Love.

Mitchell, S. A. (2020). Magic and Religion. In J. P. Schjødr, J. Lindow and A. Andrén, eds, *The Pre-Christian Religions of the North: Vol. II History and Structures, Social, Geographical and Historical Contexts, and Communication Between Worlds*. Turnhout: Brepols, pp. 643–70.

National Museum of Denmark. (n.d.). A Mysterious Crystal Ball. National Museum of Denmark. https://en.natmus.dk/historical-knowledge/denmark/prehistoric-period-until-1050-ad/the-early-iron-age/the-aarslev-grave/a-mysterious-crystal-ball.

Naylor, S. (2003). Collecting Quoits: Field Cultures in the History of Cornish Antiquarianism. *Cultural Geographies*, 10, 309–33.

Naylor, T. (2010). The Underworld of Gemstones: Part 1: Under the Rainbow. *Crime, Law, and Social Change*, 53(2), 131–58.

Nyord, R. (2020). *Seeing Perfection: Ancient Egyptian Images Beyond Representation*. Cambridge Elements. Cambridge: Cambridge University Press.

Oestigaard, T. (2020). Waterfalls and Moving Waters: The Unnatural Natural and Flows of Cosmic Forces. In R. Skeates & J. Day, eds, *The Routledge Handbook of Sensory Archaeology*. Abingdon: Routledge, pp. 179–92

Oliver, K. (2001). *Witnessing: Beyond Recognition*. Minneapolis: University of Minnesota Press.

Owens, A. (2019). The Devil or the Divine? Supernatural Objects and Multi-Period Hoards in Later Prehistory. In M. G. Knight, D. Boughton and

R. E. Wilkenson, eds, *Objects of the Past in the Past: Investigating the Significance of Earlier Artefacts in Later Contexts*. Summertown: Archaeopress, pp. 60–76.

Oxford English Dictionary (2011). Amulet. www-oed.com.ezproxy.library.sydney.edu.au/view/Entry/6778.

Pati, G. and Zubko, K. C. eds. (2020). *Transformational Embodiment in Asian Religions: Subtle Bodies, Spatial Bodies*. Abingdon: Routledge.

Paul, K. (2022). The Mayor Thinks New York Gets 'Special Energy' from Crystals. Is He Right? *Guardian* online, Thursday 9 June. www.theguardian.com/lifeandstyle/2022/jun/09/crystals-eric-adams-new-york.

Penzance Natural History and Antiquarian Society. (1888). *The Cornishman*. Thursday 9 August, p. 5.

Pétursdóttir, Þ. (2012). Small Things Forgotten Now Included, or What Else do Things Deserve? *International Journal of Historical Archaeology*, 16(3), 577–603.

Pike, S. (2001). *Earthly Bodies, Magical Selves. Contemporary Pagans and the Search for Community*. Berkeley: University of California Press.

Pinch, G. (2006 (1994)). *Magic in Ancient Egypt*. London: British Museum.

Pitarakis, B. (2022). Amulets, Crosses and Reliquaries. In E. C. Schwartz, ed., *The Oxford Handbook of Byzantine Art and Architecture*. Oxford: Oxford University Press, pp. 1–15.

Pitt Rivers Museum. (n.d.). Acorn. Used as an Amulet. [SM 26/01/2011]. http://objects.prm.ox.ac.uk/pages/PRMUID221126.html.

Posthumus, D. (2022). *All My Relatives: Exploring Lakota Ontology, Belief, and Ritual*. Lincoln: University of Nebraska Press.

Price, N. (2019) *Viking Way: Magic and Mind in Late Iron Age Scandinavia*. Oxford: Oxbow.

Pymm, R. (2017). 'Serpent Stones:' Myth and Medical Application. In C. J. Duffin, C. Gardner-Thorpe and R. T. J. Moody, eds, *Geology and Medicine: Historical Connections*. Special Publications 452. London: Geological Society, pp. 163–80.

Rider, C. (2015). Common Magic. In D. J. Collins, ed., *The Cambridge History of Magi and Witchcraft in the West: From Antiquity to the Present*. Cambridge: Cambridge University Press, pp. 303–31.

Ritchie, A. (1974). Painted Pebbles of Scotland. *Proceedings of the Society of Antiquaries of Scotland*, 104, 297–301.

Robb, J. G. (1998). The 'Ritual Landscape' Concept in Archaeology: A Heritage Construction. *Landscape Research*, 23(2), 159–74.

Samuel, G. & Johnston, J., eds. (2013). *Religion and the Subtle Body in Asian and the West: Between Mind and Body*. Abingdon: Routledge

Schmidt, O., Wilms K.-H. & Lingelbach, B. (1999). The Visby Lenses. *Optometry and Vision Science*, 76(9), 624–30.

Shally-Jensen, M. (2019). *Alternative Healing in American History: An Encyclopedia from Acupuncture to Yoga*. Santa Barbara: Greenwood.

Skeates, R. & Day, J. (2020). Sensory Archaeology: Key Concepts and Debates. In R. Skeates & J. Day, eds, *The Routledge Handbook of Sensory Archaeology*. Abingdon: Routledge, pp. 1–17.

Souza, T. P., Watte, G., Gusto, A. M., Souza, R., Moreira, J.d. S. & Knerst, M. M. (2017). Silicosis Prevalence and Risk Factors in Semi-Precious Stone Mining in Brazil. *American Journal of Industrial Medicine*, 60(6), 529–36.

Spier, J. (2018). Engraved Gems and Amulets. In R. M. Jensen and M. D. Ellison, eds, *The Routledge Handbook of Early Christian Art*. Abingdon: Routledge, pp. 141–9.

Stroh, S. (2017). The Reemergence of the Primitive Other? Noble Savagery and the Romantic Age. In S. Stroh, ed., *Gaelic Scotland in the Colonial Imagination: Anglophone Writing from 1600 to 1900*. Evanston: Northwestern University Press.

Stuckrad von, K. (2014). *The Scientification of Religion: An Historical Study of Discursive Change*. Berlin: De Gruyter.

Sutherland, P. D. (2001). Shamanism and the Iconography of Palaeo-Eskimo Art. In N. Price, ed., *The Archaeology of Shamanism*. Abingdon: Routledge, pp. 135–45.

Sutherland, A. (2009). *The Brahan Seer: The Making of a Legend*. Oxford: Peter Lang.

Taggart, D. (2018). *How Thor Lost His Thunder: The Changing Faces of An Old Norse God*. Abingdon: Routledge.

Taylor, R. L. (2014). *Deviant Burials in Viking Age Scandinavia*. Research thesis. M Phil. Institute of Archaeology: University College London. UMI U602472.

Taussig, M. (2009). *What Color is the Sacred?* Chicago: University of Chicago Press.

The Royal Household. (n.d.). Honours of Scotland. Crown Copyright. www.royal.uk/honours-scotland.

Thwaite, A. (2021). The 'Urinary Experiment': Material Evidence of Magical Healing in Early Modern England. *Magic, Ritual, and Witchcraft*, 16(1), 1–22.

Tilley, C. (2010). *Interpretating Landscapes: Geologies, Topographies, Identities. Explorations in Landscape Phenomenology 3*. Walnut Creek: Left Coast.

(2020). How Does it Feel? Phenomenology, Excavation and Sensory Experience: Notes for a New Ethnographic Field Practice. In R. Skeates & J. Day, eds, *The Routledge Handbook of Sensory Archaeology*. Abingdon: Routledge, pp. 76–93.

Trower, S. (2015). *Rocks of Nation: The Imagination of Celtic Cornwall*. Manchester: Manchester University Press.

Viestad, V. M. (2018) *Dress as Social Relations: An Interpretation of Bushman Dress*. Johannesburg: Wits University Press.

Wallis, R. J. (2003). *Shamans/Neo-Shamans: Ecstasy, Alternative Archaeologies and Contemporary Pagans*. London: Routledge.

Wallis, R. J., & Blain, J. (2003). Sites, Sacredness, and Stories: Interactions of Archaeology and Contemporary Paganism. *Folklore*, 114(3), 307–21.

Walter, D. (2001). The Medium of the Message: Shamanism as Localised Practice in the Nepal Himalayas. In N. Price, ed., *The Archaeology of Shamanism*. Abingdon: Routledge, pp. 105–19.

Weatherhill, C. (2011). *Cornovia: Ancient Sites and Cornwall and Scilly 4000BC–1000AD*. 2nd edn. Wellington: Halsgrove.

Wellcome Collection. (n.d.). Mole's Foot Amulet, Norfolk, England, 1890–1910. https://wellcomecollection.org/works/wuass8ed.

Wilby, E. (2013 (2005)). *Cunning Folk and Familiar Spirits: Shamanistic Visionary Traditions in Early Modern British Witchcraft and Magic*. Brighton: Sussex Academic Press.

Wilson, J. D. ed. (2009). William Shakespeare: *As You Like It. The Cambridge Dover Wilson Shakespeare*. Volume 3. Cambridge: Cambridge University Press.

Winter, S. (2022). The Horrors of War. *Bird Watching*. September 2022, 28–34.

White, E. D. (2014). Devil's Stones and Midnight Rites: Megaliths, Folklore and Contemporary Pagan Witchcraft. *Folklore*, 125(1), 60–79.

Yunkaporta, T. (2019). *Sand Talk: How Indigenous Thinking Can Save the World*. Melbourne: Text.

Zambelli, P. 2007. *White Magic, Black Magic in the European Renaissance: From Ficino, Pico, Della Porta to Trithemius, Agrippa, Bruno*. Leiden: Brill.

Acknowledgements

Enormous thanks to Marion Gibson for both the honour of contributing to this wonderful *Elements* series, and for her kind understanding and support when I was (repeatedly) beset by extenuating circumstances that caused a substantial delay in delivering the manuscript. I also extend my thanks to Cambridge University Press for their flexibility and support.

This manuscript would not have been possible without the astute research assistance of Dr Giselle Bader, for which I am enormously grateful. I also extend my sincere thanks to Dr Fee Mozeley for her research support during its initial stages. Finally, my heartfelt thanks to Iain Gardner for his care and encouragement throughout.

Dedicated to Mum, Janice May Johnston (1947–2022)

Cambridge Elements

Magic

Marion Gibson
University of Exeter

Marion Gibson is Professor of Renaissance and Magical Literatures and Director of the Flexible Combined Honours Programme at the University of Exeter. Her publications include *Possession, Puritanism and Print: Darrell, Harsnett, Shakespeare and the Elizabethan Exorcism Controversy* (2006), *Witchcraft Myths in American Culture* (2007), *Imagining the Pagan Past: Gods and Goddesses in Literature and History Since the Dark Ages* (2013), *The Arden Shakespeare Dictionary of Shakespeare's Demonology* (with Jo Esra, 2014), *Rediscovering Renaissance Witchcraft* (2017) and *Witchcraft: The Basics* (2018). Her new book, *The Witches of St Osyth: Persecution, Murder and Betrayal in Elizabethan England,* will be published by CUP in 2022.

About the Series

Elements in Magic aims to restore the study of magic, broadly defined, to a central place within culture: one which it occupied for many centuries before being set apart by changing discourses of rationality and meaning. Understood as a continuing and potent force within global civilisation, magical thinking is imaginatively approached here as a cluster of activities, attitudes, beliefs and motivations which include topics such as alchemy, astrology, divination, exorcism, the fantastical, folklore, haunting, supernatural creatures, necromancy, ritual, spirit possession and witchcraft.

Cambridge Elements

Magic

Elements in the Series

The Strix-*Witch*
Daniel Ogden

The War on Witchcraft: Andrew Dickson White, George Lincoln Burr, and the Origins of Witchcraft Historiography
Jan Machielsen

Witchcraft and the Modern Roman Catholic Church
Francis Young

'Ritual Litter' Redressed
Ceri Houlbrook

Representing Magic in Modern Ireland: Belief, History, Culture
Andrew Sneddon

Creative Histories of Witchcraft: France, 1790–1940
Poppy Corbett, Anna Kisby Compton and William G. Pooley

Witchcraft and Paganism in Midcentury Women's Detective Fiction
Jem Bloomfield

The Gut: A Black Atlantic Alimentary Tract
Elizabeth Pérez

The Donkey King: Asinine Symbology in Ancient and Medieval Magic
Emily Selove

Amulets in Magical Practice
Jay Johnston

A full series listing is available at: www.cambridge.org/EMGI

For EU product safety concerns, contact us at Calle de José Abascal, 56–1°, 28003 Madrid, Spain or eugpsr@cambridge.org.

www.ingramcontent.com/pod-product-compliance
Ingram Content Group UK Ltd.
Pitfield, Milton Keynes, MK11 3LW, UK
UKHW022144080726
473066UK00010B/756
9781108948791